AND 1

BALL

ALL THE BALLERS, MOVES, SLAMS, & SHINE

with
Chris Palmer

HarperResource
An Imprint of HarperCollinsPublishers

HarperCollins books may be
purchased for educational,
business, or sales promotional
use. For information please
write: Special Markets
Department, HarperCollins
Publishers Inc.,
10 East 53rd Street,
New York, NY 10022.

FIRST EDITION

Designed by
Timothy
Shaner

Palmer, Chris (Chris M.)
    Streetball : all the ballers, moves, slams, & shine / AND 1 with Chris Palmer.
    p. cm.
    ISBN 0-06-072444-7
    1. Basketball. I. AND 1 (Firm) II. Title.
    GV885.P34 2004
    796.323—dc22   2004047367

04 05 06 07 08 ❖ 10 9 8 7 6 5 4 3 2 1

Contents

CHAPTER 1

These **street poets** of the 60s and 70s spoke to thousands of followers with **artistic moves**, incalculable numbers and **Herculean feats** on the basketball court that are etched in **basketball mythology**.

History of Streetball:
The Birth of the
City Game

his hallway is long and dark. It could be a metaphor for any one of countless streetball stories. But right now it's just a hallway. It's strewn with empty 40-ounce bottles dressed in brown paper bags, their caps long since disappeared like the dreams of those who tossed them long ago. Empty Styrofoam containers from that take-out joint on 153rd lie smashed. There's a small puddle of something you take care not to step in. The air is thick in here. You can feel the souls of those who have come before you, walked these very halls. You are, in a sense, in a tunnel. One that is 17 stories above ground in the Polo Grounds Apartments in Harlem, the very same ground that once served as the ball field for the New York Giants where Willie Mays used to shag fly balls. Down one end of this tunnel is an exit sign flickering to stay alive above a door wedged open by a folded cardboard box. At the other end is a light. You walk toward it and a picture begins to form. The view is different from up here. Rooftops, clotheslines, antennas. This is 155th street in Harlem. But take a few steps closer to the window. To the light. Then look down. There it lies, a rectangular slab of asphalt painted green and red. Holcombe Rucker Park. The Rucker.

It is the Mecca of street basketball. The lifeblood of the other game began here almost 60 years ago. In 1946, a New York City Department of Parks employee named Holcombe Rucker started a basketball tournament to give neighborhood kids something to do on those muggy Harlem summer nights long before the reign of the tech, long before anyone had heard of Nino Brown and the Carter apartments. And thus, the first summer league was born.

Skinny kids with Chuck Taylors or maybe Pro Keds, knee-high three-ringed socks, and afros flowing in the breeze would pound the pavement on what quickly became the hottest hoop spot in the city, long before the game was even cool. Back then the game was a diversion, something to do so you weren't doing nothing. But cats would knock down a few jumpers not long after the Parks Department put up new nets, and before your homey could say "Lew Alcindor" the nets would disintegrate and fall off. Trouble was the city wasn't keen about replacing them, which gave rise to the lasting image of a rim with no net: the hallmark of courts of InnerCity, U.S.A. When a court has no net, as any street observer can vouch, you can forget about the outside game. The net's functional purpose is to slow the ball as it goes through the hoop. But it also provides proper depth perception when bombing from long range. Many found it too hard to adjust their games, so early streetball was about taking it strong to the hole and finishing at the rim. To do that you had to get by your man. Thus the early style of the game was born. Anyone could hoist from beyond the arc that didn't yet exist, but the game was all about putting it on the deck, the concrete, the scorching asphalt and beating your man off the dribble. There were no crossovers back then. Only change-of-direction dribbles.

The sixties in America were a time of political upheaval and the quest for equality in the face of staunch resistance—in short, instability. In the hood instability can lead to desperation, which goes hand in hand with destruction, or creative revolution. Nowhere was this epitomized better than by the early Rucker Park legends like Joe "The Destroyer" Hammond, Earl "The Goat" Manigult and Pee Wee Kirkland. These street poets of the sixties and seventies spoke to thousands of followers with artistic moves, incalculable numbers and Herculean feats on the basketball court that are etched in basketball mythology. This was hip-hop before hip-hop, long before bling and spinning rims. The NBA was not their calling, but they remain All-Harlem World and are the direct ancestors of ballers with names like Hot Sauce, Sik Wit It, and Main Event.

As the Rucker League began to gain a word-of-mouth following (the only way to get a following on the street), crowds began to number in the hundreds, then thousands. The hoods of cars and the trees that shaded Rucker became premium seating. The 155th Street bridge was the skybox. The tops of buildings were the cheap seats. If you showed up two hours early you were late.

The Rucker is where you could see the best ballers not in the league battle the NBA's best. Pros like Wilt Chamberlain, Julius Erving, Tiny Archibald, Dave Cowens, Kareem Abdul-Jabbar, Ollie Taylor, and Mike Riordan added to their legend and built their street cachet by showing up and battling street foes like Joe "The Destroyer" Hammond, Earl "The Goat" Manigault, Pee Wee Kirkland, and Fly Williams.

"What made the early streetballers so great was the fact that they had no fear of the pros," said Duke Tango, the legendary Rucker Park play-by-play MC. "They looked at the pros as just guys from the neighborhood who happened to be in the NBA. Outside of that they were just regular players to them."

Despite the fact that he never played a minute of college or NBA ball, many consider Hammond the greatest streetballer ever, the greatest king to walk any slab of asphalt ever poured for the purpose of reconfiguring Dr. Naismith's game as one's own. His high-arching jumpshot was allergic to the rim. He found driving lanes that didn't exist and his knack for scoring made it look as though he were on cruise control. He paid attention to the details as much as he did the dunks. No player from New York City ever used those metal-grated backboards as well as The Destroyer.

In 1971, the first half of the championship game of the Rucker Pro Tournament between the Milbank Hawks and the Westsiders, coached by a young *New York Daily News* basketball reporter named Peter Vecsey, was in the books when Hammond arrived just as the second half was about to start. On the other side of Eighth Avenue, Hammond stepped out of a white stretch limo and made his way through the throngs of onlookers and into Milbanks' lineup for the start of the second half. For the rest of the game he was matched up with the ABA's leading scorer, Charlie Scott, and Julius Erving, the Doctor, and dropped 50 before J could even get the pick out of his fro.

Ask Harlem residents or any hoop aficionado lucky enough to be in attendance that day and they'll say it was one of the greatest streetball games ever played. Mostly it was Joe being Joe. Casual. Aloof. Brilliant. Maddeningly confusing.

The performance led Wilt Chamberlain to talk to the Lakers about signing The Destroyer to a rookie contract. But Hammond turned down the $50,000 Lakers owner Jack Kent Cooke was offering because, he said, he could make more paper selling drugs on the street. He was right. By the time he was 21, he had over $200,000 stashed away in his apartment.

"That was real money to me," said Hammond, "Selling drugs was guaranteed money. The Lakers wouldn't even offer me a guaranteed contract."

Fifty Gs was cornstarch compared to the money he made selling marijuana and heroin when he wasn't

Joe Hammond

on the basketball court. But drive the lane enough times and you're bound to get your shit rejected eventually.

For Hammond that time came in 1971 when he was sent to prison on drug charges for 11 years. The Lakers were gone. The matchups with Dr. J were history. No more limos or mink coats or dresser drawers full of cash. Just the shell of a man who still walks the same hallowed ground he once soared over.

But Hammond wasn't the first player to use streetball to reach full-on ghetto celebrity. As a kid, Hammond idolized a six-foot sky-walker named Earl Manigault. He was nicknamed The Goat after one of his teachers mangled his last name.

They say he once took off from the foul line and got whistled for three seconds—in the air. The Goat could pluck quarters from the top of the backboard, the definitive feat of any playground legend. He was the reason anyone ever thought of something as absurd as taking anything off the top of the backboard. Then there was the time he dunked 36 times in a row. Backward. Don't sound that tough? Try it. Actually, try just touching the rim 36 times in a row.

"There are more memories of me in the air than on the ground," Manigault used to say.

Unfortunately, there were just as many memories of Goat selling, using, and doing bids. But The Goat would get it back when he went clean and opened Goat Park on 99th and Amsterdam in the late eighties, which became a haven for kids to work on their games while Goat taught them the past so they wouldn't repeat it.

In 1998, Earl died of heart failure, but to those who played with him, his memory remains as vivid as high-definition TV.

"The best player of his size in the history of New York City," said Kareem Abdul-Jabbar. "Just amazing." Kareem should know, having matched up with The Goat many times. Manigault had a knack for taking it straight at foes who were much taller. He had perfected the art of floating the ball over outstretched limbs when the defense collapsed on him. No doubt his years of going one-on-one with Kareem shaped his

Earl "The Goat" Manigault

fearlessness when confronting taller opponents on the basketball court.

And then there was Pee Wee Kirkland, who was completely ill, by all accounts. And there were many.

"The first time I saw Pee Wee, he pulls up to the Rucker Tournament in a white Rolls-Royce," said former NBA star and Rucker vet Austin Carr. "He was decked out in all white, and everyone in his posse was driving white Cadillacs. It was like he was the Pied Piper."

If he wasn't pushing a Caddy it was a Rolls. Yeah, he was something to see all right.

Iconoclastic battles took place between point gods Pee Wee and Tiny Archibald that thousands gathered to see. If you could see through the chain-link fence you had a good seat. Pee Wee looked like he was headed on the right path when he and future NBA All-Star Bobby Dandridge teamed up to lead Norfolk State to the 1968 CIAA Championship. After being drafted by the Bulls he left camp, claiming he wasn't getting a fair shake. But in 1972 he turned the ball over and got locked up on drug charges. Something to see all right.

The same is said about Connie Hawkins's aerial artistry. The Hawk was the prequel to Doc, MJ, and Vince and could cover more ground in the air than most could with a subway token. The six-eight swingman (he was swing before it was the thing) dunked on Wilt and gave a young Lew Al 40. After being wrongly accused of involvement in a gambling ring, he debuted with the Phoenix Suns and averaged 24.6 points, 10.4 rebounds, and 4.8 apg. Ahead of time with an exquisite blend of power and grace, Hawk was the Suns' Amare before Amare's parents were even born.

Along with being one of the first to play above the rim, Hawkins was the first player to cross over from the street to star in the pros.

By the time the eighties rolled around, many pros were making too much money to risk injury battling

Richard "Pee Wee" Kirkland

playground stars. Franchises weren't keen on the idea that their million-dollar investments were being put at risk. The great clashes began to fade. Stories gave way to legend, which quickly became myth. Before long the golden age of streetball had slipped past a double team and into our collective faded memory.

It seemed as though every story of one of these high-flying, colorful legends had come to a sad end in the decrepit graveyard of New York City basketball dreams. Maybe the misses stick in our minds more than the hits. But this is certain, for much of streetball's first four decades there was one formula: talent plus missed opportunity plus streets plus prison equal the downfall of another street dreamer.

Part of the reason was that back then streetball led nowhere. For a typical seventies or eighties streetballer, no matter how many points you could score in the Rucker, you were on a road to nowhere. There was no future. There was no money saved to keep your head above water, so many turned to the streets.

Very rarely, as is still the case today, does streetball performance lead to a pro contract. NBA scouts don't come to parks and gyms of the inner city to scout for talent. Back in the day nearly every NBA player was plucked directly from college basketball. At eight rounds, the draft provided the best players available. Today, high-school summer camps like ABCD and Nike, as well as major shoe company–sponsored AAU tournaments, are used to evaluate and make decisions on talent. Players who aren't in The System, for whatever reason, are already considered risks, and scouts can't be swayed by Chamberlainesque tales of players who only exist by word of mouth.

The Goat, The Destoyer, and many others like them were cautionary tales and didn't exactly help the cause of next-big-thing streetballers looking to take the alternative route to the pros. But streetball went on. All that took was a place to play and kids who loved to play. You didn't even need ten guys.

In 1982, Harlem rapper Greg Marius organized a basketball

game between the Disco Four and the Crash Crew in a hoop show-down of local MCs on 139th and Lenox. The initial showdown spawned a league—minus rappers—Marius called the Entertainers' Basketball Classic, which featured the best playground ballers, local college stars, and a smattering of pros. The league moved to its current location, Holcombe Rucker Park on 155th Street and Eighth Avenue, in the late eighties. Lloyd "Sweet Pea" Daniels, Dwayne "Pearl" Washington, Steve "All Day" Burtt, David Cain, Eric Marbury, and Richie "The Animal" Adams were a few of the players to shine during the eighties. Much like Holcombe's early Rucker Park Tournament, the EBC became the place to play for anyone with a street rep to defend or earn. Other spots like Dyckman in the Bronx and the King Dome on 116th and Lenox in Harlem were more than suitable proving grounds.

Throughout the eighties, New York's streets produced a steady stream of concrete cagers, and the street game continued unabated, but local interest lagged. The emergence of hip-hop lured some kids away from the basketball court in hopes of becoming the next LL or Rakim. Others, much like Joe Hammond, chose easy money on the streets. But even without the pitfalls of drugs and violence, the most you could get out of streetball was a reputation. Only a select few became legendary. Ballers had wandered in the concrete jungle for 40 years with nowhere to go.

But all of that was about to change.

As the nineties ushered in a new wave of streetballers—hip-hop influenced hoop artists like Tyron "Alimoe" Evans, aka The Black Widow, Malloy "The Future" Nesmith, Stephon "Starbury" Marbury, Jamal "Mel the Abuser" Tinsley, Crafton "Aircraft" Ferguson, Tim "Headache" Gittens, Junie "GE" Sanders, Todd Myles, Larry "The Bone Collector" Williams, Shane "Captain Nappy" Drisdom, Kareem "The Best Kept Secret" Reid, Richie Parker, Reggie "High Five" Freeman, Ed "Booger" Smith, and John "The Franchise" Strickland—street hoops began to experience a resurgence. One that exploded nationwide.

Top talent no longer sprang only from the five boroughs but could be found coast to coast. Washington, D.C., wasn't far behind with players who could capture the crowd's imagination, such as Lonnie "Prime Objective" Harrell, Curt "Trouble" Smith, Victor "Sky" Page, Greg "The Sorcerer" Jones, Earl "Pep" Tyson, Martyn "Moochie" Norris, Donald Ford, and Lawrence "Poetry In" Moten. But other spots repped well too, producing the likes of Robin "Sik Wit It" Kennedy (Southern California), Erron "E Money" Maxey (Southern California), Jimmie "Snap" Hunter (Memphis), Robert "50" Martin (Atlanta), and Luis "Trickz" Da Silva (New Jersey).

But it was New York's new generation who had been handed down the stories of The Goat or seen the ghost of Joe Hammond lugging a garbage bag full of bootlegs he was selling to make ends meet, or at least briefly get acquainted. These youngsters were now the stars of Rucker. Part of the new jack generation's story wasn't much different from that of their pioneering counterparts. There were still as many pitfalls outside their doors as there were cracks in 94 feet of asphalt. There were the same cold tenements. The same temptations. The same dead-end signs. Only the new kids had it worse, thanks to the violence that erupted from the crack trade that plagued the five boroughs in the eighties and early nineties.

Up to now streetball had belonged to the streets and was strictly an underground pursuit. But one player would change all that. A skinny point guard from South Jamaica, Queens, named Rafer Alston was on the verge of revolutionizing street basketball, and unknowingly would become the nexus for the globalization of the streets.

He would show them the way out.

New School: AO, Alimoe, Helicopter, Sik Wit It, Shane, The Professor, and Hot Sauce chilling in Miami, Winter '03.

CHAPTER 2

People would **take off work** to **see Skip** play. You wouldn't even take off for a Knicks game but **Skip was different**.

Like No Other:
The Story of Skip to My Lou

Know this. If not for Rafer Alston you wouldn't be reading this book. No, Skip probably didn't teach you how to read. Nor did he stuff this book in your stocking. But 10 years ago he set in motion a chain of events that changed the way you play basketball.

There's a basketball player born every night in New York City. On July 24, 1976, Geraldine Alston gave birth to Rafer Alston. She named him after Olympic decathlete Rafer Johnson. "I thought he [Johnson] was the embodiment of the black American athlete at the time," said Geraldine. "Back then Johnson gave a lot of people hope when there wasn't much hope for black people in America. For my son it just seemed fitting."

Every revolution needs a starting point. A spark. That first domino. It can come from anywhere or anybody. There is no formula, no handbook to carefully plot each point of the upheaval. Besides, grade-schoolers are usually more interested in hanging out with friends, chasing the ice cream truck, or hatching ways to stay out after the street lights come on. And Rafer Alston always played things by ear. Not that he knew what he was in for when he picked up the game of basketball as a six-year-old shorty in South Jamaica, Queens.

He got his first basketball from his mother for Christmas when he was six. The pebble grain on the surface of the ball soon became as smooth as Chris Mullin's jumpshot. He would dribble it everywhere. All day, every day. You'd be hard pressed to find a square foot of Queens asphalt that Rafer hadn't dribbled his ball on.

Geraldine loved that her son had found something so early in life that kept his mind off the temptation and trouble that existed outside the family's apartment in the American Village Apartments he shared with his older brother, Ramar, twin sister, Racine, and father, Richard. But the kid's handle wasn't so tight back then, and knocking over a lamp or two wasn't something Geraldine wanted to hear about when she got home from her job at the hospital.

He dribbled in his bedroom, the kitchen, the hallway, on the way to school, everywhere, morning, noon, and night. "The people in the apartment below asked us if we were building a bowling alley," recalled Geraldine. Then they asked the Alstons if they were planning on moving any time soon.

They weren't, so Rafer's mother took to hiding the ball in the closet or some other out-of-the-way place. But Rafer would always find it. One day she gave the ball to a family friend who ran the grocery store across the street. Rafer found out and paid the man a visit. He reluctantly returned the ball to Rafer on one condition— that he didn't tell his mother.

Back at the apartment Rafer was up to his old tricks. He took a metal hanger and fashioned it into a makeshift rim that he would hang from the top of a door. When the ceiling of his apartment could no longer contain his arching jumpshots, he moved the hanger to a light fixture in the hallway of the building for slightly high rafters.

On one not-so-swift move to the hole, the ball flew out of his hand and ricocheted off the light fixture, sending it crashing to the floor.

"I heard all this glass breaking," remembered Geraldine. "When I opened the door Rafer was gone but I knew it was him because the hanger was still hanging from the ceiling. I was so scared that the landlord was going to make us pay for it because we just didn't have the money."

Once again Geraldine took her son's beloved ball to the grocer, this time with orders not to return it. In a strange twist of fate, several years later the grocer's house burned to the ground. While sifting through the rubble, he found Rafer's basketball. Up till that point he had completely forgotten about the dribbling kid and his ball. It was the only item that survived the fire.

"Honestly, I hardly have any memories of Skip when he wasn't dribbling the ball," said his close friend and Mix Tape Tour member Troy "Escalade" Jackson.

He would always find a new ball and the dribbling continued. Rafer would tell Geraldine that he was beating an imaginary Magic Johnson off the dribble and, well, Mom wasn't trying to hear it.

"He was always playing against somebody only he could see," recalled Geraldine.

He would turn an old pillowcase into a cape and tie it around his neck and run around the Alston household calling himself Super Isiah. He'd run recklessly through the hallway shouting, "It's Super Isiah and he can't be stopped!"

"You couldn't tell him anything about Isiah," says Mike Ellis, a family friend and New York City basketball oral historian known throughout the five boroughs as Big Mike. "Isiah was by far his favorite player. Rafer would watch tape after tape; he'd just keep rewinding it until he learned exactly how Isiah did his moves. Then he'd go out and practice them."

Like most boys from Queens, Rafer also looked up to neighborhood product Mark Jackson. As a rookie with the Knicks in 1987,

Jackson was the first player credited with successfully bringing streetball-style moves to the NBA. Over-the-shoulder passes and three-card-Monte-like sleight of hand were part of Jackson's nightly act. And it worked, as Jackson was regularly among the league leaders in assists. For Rafer, the seed had been planted.

When Rafer was in the sixth grade his uncle took him to the Catholic league playoffs at St. John's. During halftime of one game, Rafer and a fifth grader named Stephon Marbury engaged in a spur-of-the-moment shooting contest. As the dueling elementary-school students drilled shot after shot, the crowd rewarded them with a rousing ovation.

Word began to spread about a wisp of a guard at PS 40 elementary school who had the ball on a string when Cardozo High School head coach Ron Naclerio began to inquire about him. Naclerio taught gym and special education at IS 8 middle school in Queens. He was a New Yorker through and through, with a gravelly voice, bigger-than-life stories, and a keen awareness of what went on in the streets. He knew the playgrounds as well as he did the AAU scene. Knew the high-school scene even better. He knew the good kids and the bad blocks as well as the bad apples and the safe hoods. Many of his opposing coaches have occasionally confused him with a snake oil salesman. Naclerio's surgeon father once removed a knife from the side of Dr. Martin Luther King, the result of a failed assassination attempt.

Rafer enrolled in IS 8 and immediately formed a bond with Naclerio. At the time, he ran a breakfast program for needy students in the morning before school. Naclerio arranged workout sessions with Rafer if he promised to show up early enough. Nearly every morning at 7:30 during Rafer's middle-school years, Naclerio put him through a series of advanced dribbling drills that would begin to shape his game.

"He already had command of the ball when I started working with him, so he wanted to go straight to fancy dribbling," said Naclerio.

They worked on a variety of dribbles: behind the back, through the legs, crossovers, and stuff Rafer would invent on the spot. Soon it became nearly impossible for anyone to steal the ball from him. He had such command of the rock that he could run at a full sprint without losing control. He was faster with the ball than others were without. On the court he could weave through defenders like a bike messenger through rush-hour traffic.

He began to scour the city looking for places to play. "If he was in Queens and there was a game in Brooklyn, Staten Island, or wherever, he was there," Naclerio said.

When he was 10, he joined a 12-and-under AAU program called Salem Young Life, coached by Dermond Player, which traveled the five boroughs throughout the summer. When he wasn't touring with Young Life he was at Rucker Park watching Naclerio coach a team called Entourage. During the middle of one game Naclerio called a timeout. When the bench players went to sit back down after the game resumed, they found it occupied by two junior-high-aged kids.

"You kids gotta get up," said Naclerio's assistant coach.

"No, they can stay," replied Naclerio. "Do you know who they are? That's Stephon Marbury and Rafer Alston, the two best young guards in the city."

At another Entourage game, Naclerio's team only dressed seven because some of his players were away at basketball camp. He had

Rafer dress just in case a few guys fouled out. In the second half, Naclerio put him in the game. Right away he took an inbounds pass and and blew by his man. Instead of pulling the ball back when he crossed halfcourt, he kept his dribble low and wrapped the ball behind his back to beat a double team. He raced into the lane and lobbed a finger roll that was promptly blocked out of bounds.

The crowd buzzed about the bold 12-year-old with a slick handle who wasn't afraid to dribble against players five and six years his senior.

"Most kids would be scared to take it to halfcourt, but Rafer took on the whole team," Naclerio said. After a couple more fancy dribbles that delighted the crowd, Naclerio pulled him out and the coach was soundly booed.

"Put shorty back in," they cried, "we want to see what he's all about."

Shorty was tough and knew the older boys couldn't take the ball from him. Rafer developed his toughness by playing against his brother, Ramar, who was 14 months older. The brothers would square off for long hours in heated sibling battles that someone usually left with tears and hard feelings.

"We'd be outside at seven in the morning and we play until four in the afternoon," said Ramar, now 28. "My game was mostly rooted in fundamentals and Rafer was into flash. We'd be playing one-on-one and he would be ahead but then he'd start doing tricks and dribble the ball out of bounds or off his leg and get frustrated."

Ramar could beat Rafer soundly for most of their adolescent lives. Then one day Rafer returned home from basketball camp to find Ramar at St. Albans Park, their main hoop spot in Queens, not including 116th and Suffolk, destroying the neigborhood regulars.

"I was just thrashing people, taking everybody's money," said Ramar. Rafer stepped up and challenged his brother to a game to 32. Pride and $50 was on the line. "I was killing him like 24–6 but he wasn't getting frustrated like usual," recalled Ramar. "All of a sudden he just took over. He just started killing me. He played a

more fundamental style of ball. When he combined it with a few tricks was when his game started to take off. The final score was 32–24, Rafer."

Dozens of high schools unofficially recruited Alston, but his mother was intent on having him attend Archbishop Malloy in Queens, one of the most respected Catholic high schools in the city. Malloy had produced NBA stars Kenny Anderson and Kenny Smith and had a legendary coach in Jack Curran, the opposite of the gruff Queens native Naclerio. Rafer, however, was dead set against it. He wanted no part of school uniforms and being separated from his friends.

Geraldine applied for Rafer's admission to Malloy despite his plea to let him go to Cardozo. A friend of Rafer's convinced Geraldine to visit the Queens school in an attempt to sway her. What she saw was a well-kept school in Bayside, an upper-middle-class neighborhood known for some of the highest math and English scores in the city. Geraldine conceded, largely due to Naclerio's insistence that he would watch over Rafer as if he were his own son. Rafer was allowed to enroll in Cardozo.

Rafer went everywhere with Naclerio. Naclerio drove Rafer all over the city to Young Life games. Naclerio's mother fixed Rafer dinner on a regular basis. He had friends keep tabs on the young point guard. When Rafer didn't come home at night, Naclerio would comb the city until he found him.

"He more or less adopted Rafer," Geraldine said of Naclerio.

By the time basketball tryouts rolled around in November, many of the 80 or so boys who went out for the team had heard of Rafer and his special connection with Naclerio. Even before he made the team he had a target on his back. "A lot of the kids, especially returning JV kids who were trying to make varsity, laughed when they first saw him," Naclerio remembered. "He was about five-eight and couldn't have weighed more than 110 pounds. He was very weak physically. A lot of the kids wanted to put him on his butt. That changed as soon a he got the ball in his hands."

His freshman year was erractic but spotted with brilliance.

Coming off the bench he averaged six points a game in 13 minutes. His season highlight was a 16-point outing against PSAL powerhouse Lincoln High in Brooklyn, home to the famous Marbury family.

In the summer following his freshman year, he began to play for Cardozo's summer league team, Dogs of War, which was coached by Naclerio. Even at 15, Rafer competed in the highly competitive 18-and-over Unlimited Division at Rucker Park. Up to that point, much like his idol Isiah, Rafer's game was rooted in fundamentals (he had learned something from his battles with Ramar). He had a penchant for flash but only if the game situation called for it. "I always stayed within myself," said Rafer. "I never really did anything that was too unnecessary."

In addition to Rucker Park, Naclerio entered his team in summer leagues throughout the city. Back then Rafer was known as The Energizer for the way he would spark a run whenever he entered a game. But when legendary Rucker Park announcer Duke Tango first saw him, he had no idea what to call him.

"No disrespect to the name Energizer but your name isn't official unless you get it from me," said Tango. "When I give you a name, you've arrived."

Rafer's first year in the Rucker was solid but not quite spectacular. Still, Tango gave Rafer a nickname.

"I called him Reeses," said Tango. "It was basically me poking fun at his name. I had never heard the name Rafer before so I just riffed on it in a playful way. I had to play with him a little bit because he was just a kid and I wanted him to feel comfortable. But I was really thinking that I didn't want him to get hurt playing with the big guys."

So that's what he was called the first of his 12 straight summers at the Rucker. Tango briefly toyed with calling him The Handler but it didn't take, so he gave it to speedy point Todd Myles. But a kid named by someone who couldn't get his name right wasn't going to change street basketball. Or maybe he was. The Goat went through the same thing. So Reeses it was and nobody suspected a revolution.

Then Rafer returned for a second summer and everything changed. The fundamentals were still ever present but there was an undeniable flash to his game. "He began to do things with the ball I hadn't seen done before," said Tango, "and I've been around a hell of a long time. His energy was different. Here was this quiet, shy kid who used to show up with a lollipop in his mouth, then proceed to electrify the crowd."

The new Rafer had an air about him that was part cocky, part innocence. His first season at Cardozo sent his confidence skyrocketing. He seemed too young to have the wherewithal to clown established stars. Or anybody, for that matter. But the brash, prodigal point guard didn't seem to have a problem with it.

On one particular play Rafer had grabbed a defensive rebound and begun to turn around to start the break when a defender reached for the ball. As the dude swiped at the ball, Rafer wrapped it around his own back in one swift motion and began to push it up court. With the crowd gasping and buzzing about the aborted theft, a burst of adrenaline surged through Rafer's body and he began to playfully skip as he crossed the midcourt line. With the ball bouncing next to him as if he were walking a dog, another defender reached for it. At the last second Rafer pulled it back with his right hand and zipped a no-look pass with his left to a teammate for the bucket. No one noticed the basket.

"I was sitting down at the time," said Tango, "and when he did it I just jumped out of my seat. The whole place erupted. Right then and there he separated himself from the rest."

Then the frenzied crowd heard one of the most memerable calls in Rucker history. "Skip, skip, skip to my Lou," shouted Tango. "Ladies and gentleman you have just seen Skip to My Lou!"

It was the street equivalent of Al Michaels's "Do you believe in miracles?" at the 1980 Olympics. Fans and street historians would recall the moment for years to come.

Tango's MCing partner Al Cash looked at Duke and said, "You've done it again."

"Done what?"

"Gave out another birth certificate."

Another streetballer was born.

"I wouldn't have believed it if I wasn't there to see it," said Big Mike Ellis. "It was a simple move but it said so much about him. And when you can excite a crowd with your personality as well as your game, that's a rare combination. And that was something that was lacking in streetball at the time. The people needed that."

The idea of a young black kid exuding a carefree demeanor despite little statistical chance at success in whatever avenue he chose in life spoke volumes, even if no one actually put it into words. The fact that he was icing foes was almost secondary.

The complexion of any ball game would change when Rafer checked in. If guys were lazily running plays, they would begin to cut hard and call for the ball. They kept their hands up on the break and defenders tightened up their footwork. They played off of him and challenged his still-suspect jumpshot, and got booed in the process. Defenders suddenly became conscious about the half-dozen or so video cameras in attendance, lest they end up like Kane and O-Dog on an oft-rewound underground nightly feature on some kid's busted-ass ghetto TV. You had to think several plays ahead of Skip, about how you were going to get him back. Because his getting you was already a given.

"I was just bringing excitement to the parks," said Skip. "I really didn't have anything in mind. Nothing was planned. It's not like I was sitting up at night dreaming of ways to clown guys or figuring out how I was going to bounce the ball a certain way. Everything I did was just a reaction to the defense, and people loved it. That's what I played for, to get the crowd involved. I wanted to get every-body hyped so they'd want to come back the next night. It was just all about entertainment."

Long after the game, people milled about talking about what

they had just seen. People who didn't see anything still went back to their blocks and told stories of how their man saw this sick dude named Skip make somebody fall or make fourteen shots in a row or something. Before Skip even got off the A train at the Utica stop in South Jamaica on his way home, the story had already begun to become mythical. Since grass doesn't grow in the ghetto, stories do.

"When I first went up there to watch him play I was floored at how many people were there," said Geraldine. "The way people reacted to Rafer was incredible. They looked at him as some kind of basketball hero, but he was just my son."

Along with Isiah Thomas, Rafer also idolized former NBA star Pistol Pete Maravich. In some of the old footage of Maravich, he would wave his hand around the ball to confuse the defender

Skip demonstrating how he got his name

before delivering a pass on the break. Skip was mesmerized by this and set out to improve on it. "What I did was wave my whole arm around the ball to add more flair," said Skip. From there he would drop the ball through his legs and throw a no-look pass with the opposite hand. No one had ever put together such a combination of moves until Skip unveiled it on a fast break in one of the countless games he played in the summer of 1994.

"People would take off work to see Skip play," said Tyron "Alimoe" Evans, the street legend from Harlem who first faced Skip at the Rucker in 1993. "You wouldn't even take off for a Knicks game, but Skip was different. You could always tell when he was there because there would be tons of traffic, cars triple parked, and thousands of people swarming 155th."

His games were so crowded, fans would spill onto the court, blurring the line between spectator and participant.

Because of Skip's ability to draw fans, the Rucker all-star game at the end of the summer was held at Riverbank State Park. There Skip broke out some of his most-talked-about moves ever in a game that featured Alimoe, the late Conrad McCrae, Half-Man Half-Amazing, Main Event, and Shane The Dribbling Machine, which fans would see a decade later in the form of Mix Tape Vol. 1.

"Very few times in life will someone come along and capture the imagination of a particular sport," said Big Mike. "In much the same way LeBron James excited people when he came into the NBA, Skip had the same effect on the street game. And once you have the hype and you deliver the goods, it increases who you are a hundredfold. That's what Rafer did."

While Skip ruled the playgrounds of New York, he could barely hold his own in the classrooms of Cardozo—mostly because he rarely visited them. Keeping him in school and thus eligible was a chore.

Naclerio took to driving Rafer to school every morning. "It was the only way I knew that he would be in school for sure," says Naclerio. "I had guidance counselors walk him to class."

In his freshman year, Skip measured in at five-eleven weighing 131 pounds. If he turned sideways you had to send out a search party. His play was erratic at times, sensational at others. He finished the season averaging just six points on 32 percent shooting but his potential had those around him eagerly awaiting the future.

"Naclerio was able to see a diamond in the rough and went out of his way to help him as a young man," said Big Mike. If Rafer was a diamond in the rough, the emphasis was on rough.

His sophomore year started out with great promise. Though Cardozo dropped its first two games, Rafer poured in 23 points, many on coast-to-coast drives, in a loss to Forest Hills. Two days later Cardozo trucked Bayside 83–33 as Skip poured in 25 points and 10 assists. Then came the 28 points in a 77–54 spanking of Springfield Gardens.

In Cardozo's sixth game of the season, Rafer notched a career-high 30 points. Then he topped that a week later with 32 in Cardozo's second Springfield Gardens game.

On February 28, 1992, Rafer played in his first-ever high-school playoff game. In the first round of the New York City PSAL playoffs Cardozo jumped out to an 18–10 lead over Forest Hills after Rafer scored 10 points in four minutes.

Skip finished with 30 but the Judges were bounced from the third round. He failed to score 20 points in only one game (19) and notched ten assists nine times. He averaged 25.2 points and led the Judges to a co–division championship in the Queens III division. After the season, observers began to whisper that Alston might have a shot to write himself into New York's storied high school hoops history if he puts together two more seasons of highly productive basketball. As Rafer would find out, that was more easily whispered than done.

His second season of high-school ball had been a success. But off the court his mother still worried about Rafer's penchant to run with some less-than-desirable crowds. She wanted Rafer out of New

York so the city's notorius distractions would have less chance to derail her son.

Geraldine read an article in *Sports Illustrated* about a prep school called Maine Central Institute in Pittsfield, Maine, for talented basketball stars who needed to relocate to less distracting environments to concentrate solely on basketball and books. She wrote the school without Rafer's knowledge to inquire about getting her son enrolled. The school's principal, Johnathan K. Alder, wrote her back in a letter dated May 11, 1992, which read in part:

> *Mrs. Alston,*
> *Thank you for your interest in Maine Central Institute. We offer several exciting opportunities and are delighted to know you are eager to learn more about our community. It's my hope that we can fulfill your son's academic needs. We'll be in touch.*

"Sometimes when you come from backgrounds like Rafer's you have to sacrifice a little more to get where you want to go," said Geraldine. "At the time my son wasn't willing to do that."

Rafer had no interest in the tiny, remote school and stayed in Queens. "It's too cold up there," is what he told his mother. He began his junior year at Cardozo in torrid fashion. On December 10, 1992, he recorded the school's first-ever quadruple double with a line that read like an egregious misprint: 33 points, 10 rebounds, 11 assists, and 13 steals.

The good times wouldn't last. Six days later when report cards came out, Rafer was declared academically ineligible for the first time in his career. He was averaging 28.5 points in a remarkable 18 minutes per game.

The local New York media were all over the story of Rafer's ineligibilty. Each day Geraldine would cringe at stories about how her son's nonchalance toward school and family problems led to his not being able to make the grade.

"That was a bit much," said Geraldine. "People didn't realize that Rafer was just 16 years old, and it affected him to see his name in the paper in a negative light so often. He was at the age where he was just beginning to be social and go out and he didn't want everyone to know that he failed calculus everywhere he went. Where was he going to go? Was he going to hide in the house until things blew over? Those were hard times because people treated my son like he didn't care about anything in life."

"This child does not belong to the newspapers," she told *Newsday* in 1993. "He does not belong to the coaches. I gave birth to this child and the fact is that no one would give a damn about this child if he didn't play basketball. He would be just another inner-city black child."

In the summer following his junior year, the summer of 1993, Skip attended the Nike ABCD camp in Ypsilanti, Michigan. Street and Smith High named him high honorable mention. That summer a New York–based filmmaker named Danielle Gardner followed Rafer around the city with a camera crew to gather footage for a basketball documentary called *Street Ball*. But Rafer's footage was eventually shelved in favor of the exploits of Brooklyn star Ed "Booger" Smith and his summer team, Kenny's Kings. The movie was released in 1999 under the title *Soul in the Hole*.

Still, there wasn't a kid in any borough who knew the subways better than Skip. In the summer he would sometimes travel from Queens to Rucker to Dyckman and back playing in four games a day, as many as he would play in his entire senior year at Cardozo.

By this point in his life Rafer had developed no love affair with school. The kid had a habit of sleeping in late and didn't begin going to class regularly until October.

"It got to the point that I doubted if I wanted to do this or not," Rafer told *Newsday* in 1993. "I wouldn't mind going to college and not even playing ball. I want to make the NBA, but now it looks like I won't even be close. But I got to go to school and pass my classes and at least graduate. This is not something I can't undo. I can undo it. But is it something I want to undo? I'm not sure."

"I was very, very angry with Rafer," said Geraldine. "He was 17, looked 15, and acted 13."

When Skip finally stepped on the basketball court as a senior, his ability was mind-blowing. He scored 33 points a game in just 17 minutes of play. But as hot as he was on the court, he was invisible off it and was suspended for not having enough classes.

"Some days, I was just absent," Rafer told the *New York Times* in 1994. "I don't know; it's just me. I told Coach, 'I'm getting lazy,' and Coach would get mad. Some days, I just stayed home. My mother and father screamed at me. She'd find me at 12 noon, and school was like over. One day would lead to another and another."

A temporary restraining order let Rafer play in four games—he averaged 30.2 points, 9.7 assists, and 7.1 rebounds in 19.5 minutes per game—but then he lost his eligibility for good.

In January of his senior year, Skip's high-school career was over.

"I was up there with Stephon Marbury and Felipe Lopez, but I never had a full high-school career to show my talent," said Rafer, with his usual smile. "The difference is they went to class, I didn't."

He left Cardozo and a month later was enrolled at Laurinburg Institute in North Carolina, which Earl Manigault once attended to get away from New York. But like The Goat, Rafer was back in New York in about six weeks. (Other high-profile Laurinburg attendees included Chris Washburn and Lloyd Daniels.)

He then got his GED before heading out west to Ventura Community College in Ventura, California, an hour north of Los Angeles.

"I learned a lot from that experience," said Rafer. "I learned how to become a real point guard. We ran a lot and there were situations where I would normally throw a fancy pass and Coach Matthews would get on me about keeping it simple. He wanted me to understand that there was a different way to play the game."

In his first college game he had 2 points and 13 assists. "Coach even made me pass to a guy who was so nervous he had a bloody nose," Rafer said. With Skip running the ship, Ventura won the

California junior college state championship and finished 37–1. He averaged 9.9 points, 6.2 assists, and 2.5 steals and was named MVP of the tournament.

Rafer transferred to Fresno City Community College the following year, after a falling-out with the coach, but sat out to get his academics in order. He was eligible the following year and averaged 17.3 points, 8.6 assists, and 2 rebounds in 32 games as a sophomore in the 1996–97 season. That spring he finally signed with a four-year school. He would be the starting point guard for Jerry Tarkanian's Fresno State Bulldogs.

"I just wanted to do what I had to to get in the NBA," said Skip. "I've always considered myself a serious ballplayer, not a trickster, and college was the way to go."

It was a step in the right direction.

To see more of SKIP, check out:
- AND 1 Mix Tape Vol. 1
- AND 1 Mix Tape Vol. 2
- AND 1 Mix Tape Vol. 3
- AND 1 Mix Tape Vol. 4
- AND 1 Mix Tape Vol. 5
- Skip vs. Alimoe Battle Tape
- AND 1 Ball Access: The Mix Tape Tour
- Season 1 of ESPN's StreetBall: *The AND 1 Mix Tape Tour*
- Season 2 of ESPN's StreetBall: *The AND 1 Mix Tape Tour*

CHAPTER 3

Skip and AND 1 basically **built professional streetball from the ground up.** Without them it does not exist.

How AND 1
Took Streetball
Global

on Naclerio kept in touch while Rafer was in school out west. In New York he did what he could to steer some pub toward the best player he'd ever coached. In the spring of 1997 Naclerio dropped off a tape at the offices of *Slam* magazine in New York City. Over the years he had collected hours of footage of Rafer tearing up the Rucker and other leagues around New York, and he compiled the best on a single tape.

The wobbly pre-steady-shot footage defined amateur video. But all the production values in Hollywood couldn't have made what was captured more intriguing. Rafer put the ball in places it had never gone before. The way he zipped it from point A to point B had people rubbing their eyes in disbelief.

"We watched it a ton and were pretty blown away with what we saw," said *Slam* editor-in-chief Russ Bengtson. "Most of us had never heard of Skip before so right away it piqued our interest. We knew we had to do something with him."

In nine years, *Slam,* an NBA-heavy monthly, had put only two college basketball players on its cover, let alone one who had never even played D1 ball. But *Slam* featured Rafer in its college basketball preview issue in December of 1997 and put Skip on the cover. The headline boldly declared, "The Best Point Guard in the World (you never heard of)."

"People looked at us like who the hell is this kid," said Bengtson. "Now people were talking about him and checking the schedule to see if Fresno State came on ESPN2 or something. Almost right away people wanted to know who he was."

(In an odd piece of the magazine's history, a year earlier they had run a picture of Skip at Fresno City touting him as one of the top ten JUCO players in the country. The picture they ran showed Rafer with braided hair. Still furthering Skip's street cred, the shot is believed to be the first-ever published photo of a ballplayer wearing cornrows.)

"That cover was big for me because I was starting to get recognition for playing legitimate basketball," said Rafer. "The other thing it did was put a target on my back. Everybody we play against at Fresno was after me because I was on the cover of *Slam.*"

If exposure was what Rafer wanted at Fresno, he got it. And then some. Fresno gave permission to a film crew to document every moment of the Bulldogs' 1997–98 season. The result was "a horrendous disaster," said Rafer's mother, Geraldine. "Those boys were crazy. I didn't enjoy seeing that."

The team endured one debilitating setback after another. If it wasn't center Avondre Jones being twice suspended for marijuana use, it was fabled guard Chris Herron entering rehab in the middle of the season. Rafer also drew criticism for his arrest after an altercation with an ex-girlfriend and a car crash he was in after he fell asleep at the wheel.

"I though it was all over," he said of the late-night crash. "I thought, man, is this the way it's going to end?"

The Bulldogs fought through a tumultuous season to finish

18–12 and secure a berth in the National Invitational Tournament, with the finals being held at Madison Square Garden, where they lost to Minnesota 91–89.

"Being back home and playing in the Garden was special," said Skip. "After all I've been through, to be on that floor was something I'll never forget."

Skip had played well and gotten the national shine he was looking for. He left Fresno after his junior year and was drafted by the Milwaukee Bucks with the 39th pick of the 1998 NBA draft.

"Rafer the legit ballplayer made it to the league," said Geraldine, "not Skip to My Lou the streetball legend."

The editors at *Slam* encouraged Naclerio to show his tape around. When he gave the tape to folks at AND 1, their reaction was similar to that of the *Slam* editors. The small sneaker company in Paoli, Pennsylvania, was set on capturing the street market. They were the anti-Nike, which thrived on Madison-Avenue-inspired advertising campaigns to reach mainstream America. AND 1 wanted to take the message straight to the ballers on the playground. The company began out of the back of business student and avid pickup baller Seth Berger's car when he sold trash-talk T-shirts to fellow hoopers.

AND 1 saw itself as the voice of the true street players, the everyday pickup baller who was passionate about playing hoops.

When the tape began to circulate throughout the office, desks emptied as people gathered in the employee lounge and daily tripped off what they dubbed the Skip Tape. They couldn't get enough of it and neither could others.

A year later AND 1 was set to film a series of television commercials when they flew in some of their NBA endorsers, including Darrell Armstrong, Rex Chapman, and Larry Hughes, who passed time watching the Skip Tape over and over again between takes. Pros were mesmerized by the skinny stranger one-upping Maravich's ingenuity and turning conventional passing wisdom on its ear.

AND 1 knew it was time to go public. They edited the highlight tape, added special remixes, called it Mix Tape Vol. 1, and churned out 50,000 copies. They made an arrangement with FootAction shoe stores to distribute the tape. If you bought something at FootAction, you got the tape. They moved 200,000 in three weeks. People bought stuff they didn't need just so they could get the tape.

"It seemed that kids from nearly every neighborhood in America had the tape," said Rafer's former agent Keith Kreitor, who originally signed Skip to AND 1. "People went nuts for Rafer from that point on."

This was the beginning of something, but they didn't exactly know what. They were sure of one thing: A second tape had to be made. Since they had called the first installment Vol. 1, they were all but expected to release a followup. They needed footage and fast.

So with the help of street dunker Waliyy "Main Event" Dixon, AND 1 organized a game in Linden, New Jersey, and handpicked six of the best streetballers they could find. The original six were Dixon, Malloy "Future" Nesmith, Shane "The Dribbling Machine" Woney, Anthony "Half-Man Half-Amazing" Heyward, Crafton "Aircraft" Ferguson, and Tim "Headache" Gittens. They threw in some Jersey locals and the game was on.

It was a smash. Two thousand people packed the outdoor court, witnessed Main Event leap over a motorcycle for a dunk, and were treated to an up-tempo fan-friendly style of ball that had more tricks than Hollywood Boulevard. Mix Tape Vol. 2 is composed mainly of footage from the Linden game. When Vol. 2 shot out of stores more quickly than its predecessor had, they were on to something.

A few months later Skip and Main Event helped organize the Platinum Player game at Hunter College in Manhattan on October 31, 1999. The footage provided much of the content of Mix Tape Vol. 3 and showed AND 1 the potential when it came to holding organized streetball games. The line was down the block and around the corner despite frigid conditions. Rapper Mos Def ripped at a post-game miniconcert and AND 1's camera captured every moment on tape.

(Top Row) Larry Hughes, High Octane, Eric Holmes, Shawn Marion, Tyrone Nesby, Reggie Cotton, Milt Palacio, (Bottom Row) Hot Sauce, Sik Wit It, AO, and Skip, Venice Beach, 2002

"Afterward we all looked at each other in amazement and said, 'This is it, we have something here, let's blow this up,'" said former AND 1 marketing director Jeff Roth.

The game gave birth to the Mix Tape Tour.

In the summer of 2000, the initial Mix Tape Tour was a three-city, seat-of-your-pants jaunt that stopped in Los Angeles, Chicago, and Atlanta and tried to mimic the magic of the Platinum Player game.

The LA game was held at Southwest College in South Central where the LA Clippers practiced. The players wore T-shirts (sometimes skins) in games that were raggedy but highly entertaining affairs.

The crowd was a blend of Mix Tape die-hard fans and curious onlookers who wanted to decide for themselves whether the games were legit.

"People wanted to see if what we did was real," said AO. "They had seen Mix Tapes 1 and 2 and some had their doubts about how authentic it was. After they saw us, it didn't take long for them to realize it was legit."

Flash, Alimoe, and Reggie Cotton relaxing on the AND 1 bus—LA, 2002

Alimoe, Flash, Skip, Half-Man, High Octane,
New York City, 2002

The team did its own promotions, stapling signs to telephone poles and canvassing college campuses with fliers announcing the world's best streetball players.

"Whenever we went to the mall or went to go get something to eat we got the word out about the tour," said AO. "People looked at us like we were crazy but we had to spread the news."

Back then there wasn't the caravan of six tour buses there is today. The team was driven around in a black Ford Expedition by its announcer, DJ Set Free. Sometimes they would stop by radio stations with call-in hip-hop shows or drive to the nearest black college.

The following year the tour expanded to five cities in which games would be played and 11 others where the team would hold demonstrations. By July 2001, streetball had mushroomed into a phenomenon.

The game in Philadelphia that year was held at a local hoop hot spot at the corner of 16th and Susquehanna in North Philly, where an overflow crowd of 5,000 brought back memories of Rucker Park in Joe Hammond's heyday.

Kids lined the roof of a nearby elementary school, their legs dangling off the edge. Shaky fire escapes supported dozens of would-be fans as no one seemed to notice the bolts coming loose at the hinges. One kid climbed 25 feet up a tree and needed the fire department to get him down.

By the end of the 2002 Tour, AND 1 could no longer control the massive crowds and decided to move the show indoors to mostly NBA arenas around the country. In some cities the Mix Tape Tour would fill more seats than the local NBA team. In 2003, AND 1 began holding open runs during the day before the featured game to gauge whether any local talent had what it took to run with the world's best. Local streetballers who think they've got what it takes to run with the big boys show their skills in pickup games presided over by Mix Tape Tour members. The three best locals are chosen to run in the main game with the Mix Tape team. At the end of each game AND 1 chooses one of the three players who has survived to play in the next game. It's streetball meets *American Idol*. At the end of the tour the last man standing wins a contract and becomes the newest member of the Mix Tape Tour. The first-ever contest winner was point guard Grayson "The Professor" Boucher of Salem, Oregon, who in 2003 outlasted ballers from over 30 cities to become an official Mix Tape team member.

By 2003, the original Skip Tape had mushroomed into a streetball industry with an ESPN documentary called *Streetball*, one of ESPN's high-rated original shows, a video game featuring the Mix Tape ballers, and a 33-plus city international tour with stops in Paris, Barcelona, London, Milan, and Frankfurt. AND 1 streetballers are regularly featured in nonbasketball national ad campaigns selling everything from chips to soda.

"You better believe everybody making a living off of streetball, not just the players but everybody taking in money better pay homage to Rafer," said Kreitor.

"Sometimes I think about the old streetball players that didn't make it, like The Goat and Joe Hammond," Rafer offered. "There are so many of them and I keep them in mind. People look at me as the one who made it but I proved I could do a lot of things. I played at a major college and ran a team. I didn't make it to the league off of Rucker or because I could bounce the ball off of somebody's head or because I know somebody. It's hard work and there is no way around that. But if other guys can get some shine that's great."

"Skip and AND 1 basically built professional streetball from the ground up," said *Slam* editor Russ Bengtson. "Without them it does not exist."

"Skip is the one who revitalized streetball," Big Mike boomed. "When it wasn't as popular in the late eighties to the early nineties he gave it that spark and made people on the local level interested the way they were in the sixties when Goat and Joe Hammond used to play. Streetball is where it is now because of how Rafer Alston played the game."

Like no other.

CHAPTER 4

Because I **could throw** the ball between guys' legs and handle it **real well** people became interested in me. I went from **Ali-who to Alimoe**.

The Ballers:
The AND 1 Mix Tape Team

hey come from hoop hotbeds and they come from nowhere. They come from places as diverse as the blacktop of New York City, the suburbs of rural Oregon, and the sweltering humidity of Washington, D.C. They're branded with names like Hot Sauce, Sik Wit It, and Main Event. They are the 15 best streetball players in the world. Some of them have tasted the big-time. Others have shown their stuff on the college level. All of them have dominated, and in some cases reinvented how the game is played on the streets.

"Not everyone can identify with playing in the NBA, college, or even high school," says Aaron Owens, better known as AO on the street. "But playing streetball or pickup ball is something everyone can identify with. That's a level every single person has played on."

Beneath the style and flash of their moves lies a competitor's heart. "We play basketball to win," says Troy "Escalade" Jackson. "If we entertain in the process that's just part of the package."

Each member of the AND 1 Mix Tape Team has traveled a different, sometimes obstacle-filled road to make it to the top of today's streetball world. This is the first wave of international streetball stars. Like those of their NBA counterparts, their moves and personalities are known to fans from Seattle to Madrid, Houston to Sydney, Chicago to Paris, and all points in between.

They say everyone's got a story to tell.

These are their stories.

Tyron "Alimoe" Evans
Black Widow
TOUR DEBUT: 2002

The kid had more nicknames than just about anybody. Alimoe, Crispy Al, Rock Head, Alibaba and the 40 Thieves, Ethiopian, Black Widow. It seems just about everybody he came across in his first 27 years in Harlem tabbed him with a new nickname. His grandmother, best friends, dope dealers, Duke Tango, and dudes he didn't even know all handed him a new handle within minutes of meeting him and seeing his trademark smile, easygoing personality, and sick handle.

Mix Tape Vol. 1 caught fire because of the moves of Rafer Alston. But spliced in between all of Skip's highlights was the slick work of an unknown six-seven skinny guard who could handle the ball like he was six-one. "People were like who that dark-skinned kid doing all that stuff," recalled Alimoe. "Outside of Harlem nobody had any idea who I was.

"Because I could throw the ball between guys' legs and handle it real well people became interested in me. That was about the time I really became known on the streets. I went from Ali-Who? to Alimoe."

No matter what you call him, he started out Tyron Allan Evans and grew up in a fifth-floor apartment on 140th and Lexington in Harlem. His bedroom window gave him a perfect veiw of Lexington Avenue Park, the courts where he learned to play ball. On most summer days as a kid he would rise before eight and be out on the blacktop by himself in 90-degree heat.

His mother would be off to her job by 4:30. She would leave instruction with Al's aunt not to let him play ball in the morning sun, but everyday passersby would see the little kid dribbling back and forth and hoisting awkward jump shots.

Nate Myers, one of the older boys in his building, walked by one morning and called him Crispy Al because he was sure to burn up under the morning sun. The kid had his first nickname and he couldn't even touch the net.

Back then they used to run Rucker games at LA Park. In the summer of 1986, 11-year-old Al watched courtside as Dominique Wilkins squared up with a street legend named Rudy Myers. Dominique dunked the ball so hard the screws fell out of the rim.

The street flowed with trouble but Al loved Harlem from the go. When he went to South Philly or Athens, Georgia, to visit family it felt as if the world slowed down. His cousins in Georgia couldn't believe his moves or the fact that just about everybody in Harlem could do them, too. Guys who weren't even ballplayers would leave their jobs selling newspapers on the corner and ball for two hours and you'd think they were Rucker regulars. When cousins came to visit they couldn't believe the energy Harlem exuded. The block would be packed at one in the morning. Stores would still be open. Clubs were booming. Rappers were walking down the street and hanging out in barbershops like everybody else.

"It's nothing to walk out of your house and see Damon Dash on one block and Puff on the next," said Al. "When I brought Sauce up there he couldn't believe it."

When he wasn't stargazing at LA Park, he followed his older brother Lamar "Stick Ice" Evans and his cousins John and Ron Arnold, who later went to Xavier and Rice, respectively, to Rucker Park on 155th where they'd face Chris Mullin and Mark Jackson. Lamar went to Tolentine High School in the Bronx, where he was a teammate of the late NBA star Malik Sealy. Alimoe also spent time hanging out ten blocks south on 145th and Lenox where the

Chick All-Star Tournament was host to legendary battles between Walter Berry and Richie "The Animal" Adams.

Kenny Anderson, who went to Archbishop Malloy in Queens and was the most heralded NYC prep in 30 years, would often stay nights at the apartment of Al's cousin John. Once Al and his boy John Electric (because he could electrify the crowd) were at a bus stop when Anderson spotted him. Electric ran to the next block and told everyone he could find that Al knew Kenny Anderson.

"When I was young there was nothing you could tell me, because I was from Harlem," he mused. "Growing up here, I've seen everything. I've seen Joe Hammond and The Goat in my neighborhood. I've seen Michael Ray Richardson and Kenny Anderson. I've seen Bill Clinton and Mike Bloomberg. I've seen Snoop. There's dudes from Cali who ain't seen Snoop yet. There's not a place in the world where they ain't heard of Harlem."

"They had everything in Harlem," said Queens-born Rafer Alston. "They had the Rucker, the best clothes, the best jewelry, the flashiest cars. You couldn't tell them that they weren't the ultimate."

Harlem is also where he

made friends, some of whom who were destined for big things. Two buildings down lived a young baller named Cameron Giles, who later became known to rap fans as Cam-ron. Al and Cameron's mothers were friends, so the boys became tight by association. "Cam always had to be in the house by five o'clock," remembered Al. Six blocks up lived the future rapper Mase, whom they called R2-D2 because he talked so slow. When the boys were 11 and 12 they played for a 13-and-under AAU team called Young Life coached by Dermond Player.

Back then Cameron had the most advanced game of the three. He paid attention to both ends of the floor, Mase specialized in the little things, and Al could already handle the ball with the best of them. Together they were trouble. Young Life won nearly every tournament in the Bronx, Brooklyn, Queens, and Manhattan. One summer they dispatched the Gauchos, an AAU power, whose starting point guard was Stephon Marbury.

When they weren't on the basketball court they could usually be found somewhere on Lex doing what kids do. In the mornings they would take turns gathering at each other's apartments and hooking up a breakfast of biscuits, eggs, and toast in a scene right out of *Juice*. When they had somewhere to go, they would all hop the subway turnstile because usually they had no money. When they were hungry again, Cam would go into a deli and come out with a bag of chips for each of his boys. From there it was off to the 125th Street movie theater to buy one ticket each and stay all day. Often they were joined by Shamgod Wells, a future star point guard at Providence, who would dribble so low to the ground that defenders would scrape their hands on the asphalt trying to steal the ball from him.

As the boys got older they began taking their five to projects around the city looking for a game. Be it 112th or Grant Projects or the King Dome, they ran there. After runs at Dyckman in the

Bronx, they would walk home if a cop was on duty at the subway booth and they couldn't hop the train. "Everyone knew us," said Al, "people used to be like there goes snotty-nosed Mase, Crispy Al, and Dirty Sham. They used to make songs about us.

"We were all together. All we had was each other. We didn't have money. We didn't even know what money was. Only people in the hood who had money were the dealers. If my mom gave me 10 dollars then we were rich. We'd head straight for the Chinese joint, get takeout and two big 50-cent sodas. That was our life and we loved it."

Along the way he was still picking up nicknames. But when he tried to get a job through New York City's Summer Youth Employment Program, the city didn't know what to call him. He wrote Allan Evans on the job application but his birth certificate read Tyron Evans. The city denied him a job.

By high school the group began to go their separate ways. Cam and Mase joined prep sensation Richie Parker at Manhattan Center. Shamgod left for LaSalle Academy downtown and Al went to Julia Richman Educational Center, one of the poorest high schools in the city.

In Al's junior year, Richman faced the Cardozo Judges and their dynamic but seldom-seen point guard Rafer Alston. The previous summer Al and Skip had faced off at Rucker Park and Riverbank gym in what would later become the basis for the Skip vs. Alimoe tape. But this was high-school ball and the venue was the FIT, host to the 1992 Gobbler Classic. Midway through the first quarter Rafer drove the lane and was fouled hard by Richman point guard Vic Jordan. Jordan's and Alston's tempers flared and the two guards engaged in a clumsy shoving match while spewing junk in each other's ears.

Alimoe came to Jordan's aid and shoved Alston aside. The referee tossed Alimoe, crushing Richman's chances of winning. Adding to Alimoe's woes, the official ordered him to go to the top of the bleachers and sit with his back to the game. Al sat and faced the wall for three quarters to the jeers of fans as Cardozo drove his team into the ground.

The following year the team had a deep roster and high expectations to match. Anchored by the triumvirate of Alimoe, Virgil Smiley, and Courtney "Pooter" Miles, Richman figured to be one of the strongest squads in the PSAL. And they were. They had two plays that no defense could answer—Ram Right and Ram Left. Call Ram Left and the left-handed Miles got the ball on the left wing free to create. Ram Right was meant for Alimoe on the right side.

"There were games where I'd have 41 and he'd have 42," said Alimoe. "We were 40–40 before Jay-Z."

His best effort came against John Adams High as Alimoe rang up 45 points and 20 rebounds in the second game of the year.

That year Alimoe redeemed himself at the Gobbler by taking advantage of Cardozo while an academically ineligible Rafer sat courtside. Richman won easily, running their record to 9–1, and Alimoe won the Gobbler MVP. During the tournament Evans ran into Stephon Marbury's father, Don, there watching his son play. Don encouraged him not to waste his skills and told him they would look into possibly getting Al a ride to Georgia Tech, where Stephon had just committed. Things were looking up.

But there was a touch of bad news. Late in the Cardozo game he caught an elbow above his eye and a golf-ball-sized knot kept him out of school for the next two days. While at home with an ice pack on his head, he got a phone call from the school. A Richman administrator told him that he had been ruled ineligible because of his status as a fifth-year senior. The school had to forfeit all nine wins. His high school career was over just like that.

He watched Marbury from Coney Island's Lincoln High and Felipe Lopez of Manhattan's Rice, the two best players in the country, get more publicity and attention from college scouts because they were willing to work.

"I never thought I was as good as Felipe, because I knew he worked harder than I did," said Alimoe. "Even Cam and Richie

Parker at Manhattan Center had discipline, because their coach preached it. But I always knew that I couldn't go to a real school because that required discipline and they just wouldn't put up with me. I just wanted to be free."

So free he was. The summer after high school he debuted at Rucker, where there were no coaches to tell him to run stairs, be on time, or hold early morning practices. "I knew back at the time I wasn't making the right decision but I didn't care because it was the easiest and most fun road I could take. I liked things to be easy. I was just plain lazy back then. Even still, if I would have only had the common sense to know hard work pays off things might have turned out differently."

Being popular in the neighborhood was intoxicating. So was getting paid to play in the Rucker by dealers who simply wanted bragging rights that they could put together better teams than anyone else. At 19, he became a neighborhood celebrity. He signed autographs before, after, and during games. In one game that first summer, against the Flava Unit, Alimoe put the ball behind his back on the break, then crossed over from left to right so fast that his man got completely twisted around and droppped to the pavement.

A fan was so amazed he threw his hat onto the court and asked Alimoe to sign it. He would even get paid in the winter six months before the games began. All of a sudden girls wanted to know if he was available. He couldn't walk one block in Harlem, at any hour, without having at least five people shake his hand or blow the horn from a passing car.

"People would just buy me clothes and whatever I wanted just so they could be associated with Alimoe," he recalled. "I had Jordans, Versace shades, and gold chains. In Harlem, whenever you're the best at something, you can survive. Whether you're a rapper, basketball player, dancer, or whatever, someone will pay you because they want bragging rights. I was the best baller on the street so I survived for 25 years without a job."

After high school, he accepted an offer to play JC ball at Sullivan County College in Loch Sheldrake, New York, an hour and a half north of Harlem. On a trip home during his freshman year he met a local girl named Shila Jones. Al had always known about Jones. She went to school with Cam, Mase, and Richie Parker at Manhattan Center. Right away he felt the need to impress. "I just started lying to her saying I was going to the NBA and I'm going to be rich," he remembered. "I tried to get her with basketball because everything I've ever gotten in my life was through basketball. I didn't know any other way."

Shila didn't know much about hoops, but since they knew some of the same people it made for good enough conversation for him to get her phone number.

He pulled out all stops to impress her. He was 18 years old and smack in the middle of an identity crisis. "I was walking around listening to 2Pac, cursing, wildin' out, just not being me," he said. "But she saw right through that."

"One minute he was talking about how much he loved his mother," said Shila. "The next he was quoting 2Pac and trying to act crazy."

Shila figured there had to be more to him than that. The two grew closer but stayed away from a romantic relationship. She cooked him meals, helped him with his schoolwork, and talked to him about things other than basketball. The interaction began to take effect. He stopped cursing and smoking, shed his hangers-on, changed the way he dressed, and began to feel better about himself.

"I never met somebody who liked me for Al," he said. "I always bragged about basketball to get people to like me. I mean, I had family members that didn't care about me the way she did. She cried when I didn't go to class because she knew I was hurting myself. She wanted me to go to class more than my coach."

A year later he was out of Sullivan and back in Harlem. Basketballwise, he didn't get much out of it but at least he met Shila.

Back before the tour started, when AND 1 was organizing a game at 4th Ward Park in Linden, New Jersey, to put together footage for what would become Mix Tape Vol. 2, Alimoe was nowhere to be found. "I was 21 and I wasn't tryin' to hear about AND 1," said Alimoe. "Back then it was not what it is now. Those guys weren't even getting paid. I had guys taking care of me financially to play at Rucker and that was more important to me."

Then a year later, in 2000, the fledgling AND 1 Mix Tape Tour stopped off at Riverbank on the Upper West Side. Al took his nephew, who wanted to see Future and Skip, but had no intention of playing himself. AND 1's Mark Edwards saw Alimoe in the crowd and asked him to play on the opposing team. He took the invitation and ended by nearly stealing the show. After that it was back to Rucker and the under-the-table cash.

One day during the winter of 2000, Alimoe was sitting in his mother's apartment on 146th St. in Harlem contemplating if he would ever get paid legitimately to play basketball. His other choice was school. The streets weren't an option. They were out there but Al knew they led nowhere.

"I thought I can't be as good as the streets hyped me to be if nobody's paying me to play basketball," said Alimoe. "I know I'm better than other cats, so why was I being ignored?"

For years before that realization that day in his mom's apartment, Alimoe battled issues of self-worth and was burdened by other people's inflated perception of him. He feared the day he would have to put down the basketball for good.

"That day at my mom's I was hanging by the last bar," he recalled. "I was in a deep hole mentally. I was disturbed at my lack of success. I mean, I knew life was tough but I couldn't understand why things were so hard for me."

It would only get worse.

To get his mind off a life that had come to a halt, Al headed for Kennedy Center gym to do the one thing that brought him solace without fail—play basketball. The run that day was fast

and physical. Lenny Cooke was running things till Alimoe got his burn. Cooke could do nothing with Al's back-and-forth crossover. Shot after shot, ooh after aah, the ghetto celebs battled. About an hour into the run Al dove for a loose ball and hyperextended his left knee when he awkwardly planted his foot. The pain killed.

After he got home he showered, changed, and was about to cook himself dinner when nature called. Sitting there on the commode, he looked at his knee and what he saw put a knot in his stomach. It had swollen to the size of a grapefruit and appeared to be out of joint, protruding awkwardly out to the left.

He went into the other room, sat down, put his head in his hands, and started to cry. This was surely the end of Alimoe.

"Why are all these bad things happening to me?" he wondered aloud through tears. "I'm not a bad person but all of this bad stuff was happening to me. You can't find 10 people in Harlem to say anything bad about me. I had luck but it was all bad. Man, I knew drug dealers who had better luck than me."

He took tons of pills and went through bags of ice and heat to treat the knee. Evans even took to wearing a knee brace for the first time in his life even when he walked around. After four days of being cooped up in his mother's apartment, he again, if purely out of habit, went to the gym to play ball.

The usual crowd of talented, nicknamed no-names were there. Alimoe hesitantly called next and before long was finishing the break with two-hand flushes and slicing up the lane as if it were August at Rucker Park. In the middle of the game he stopped and looked down at his knee—he had forgotten to wear the knee brace.

"It was like God came down and healed me," declared Evans.

But still, the problem of what he was going to do with his life wasn't going away. "It was just so sad to think of myself without basketball," he said. "Was I done at 26? Was that it? My entire life people associated me with basketball. Who's Alimoe? He's that kid who plays ball. Nothin' else. He don't do no dirt, he just plays ball. Who am I going to be if I'm not in the gym shaking somebody?

"All people ever did was constantly tell me I should be making it to the league. I was so nice at 15, people looked at me now and acted like there was something wrong with me because I was still struggling. They made me think that as long as I could breathe and dribble that I should be trying to make the league. They made me believe that I was nothing, nobody if I stopped playing basketball and went back to school or got a regular job or some-thing. It took me turning 27 to believe that wasn't true, but that's how people look at you if you're from Harlem and you can play ball."

Shila confirmed to Al that she would love him the same if he worked in a post office or at Office Depot. He didn't have to be a basketball star. Mom reinforced it, too. "When they told me that it just took a load off my shoulders," said Al. "Around them I felt like a normal person. I didn't constantly have to prove myself to them the way I had to people on the streets or in basketball."

The most plausible option was going back to school to earn a degree in criminal justice, which he originally planned to do when he reached his mid-thirties, well after his competitive playing days were over. Then there was the matter of paying for school, something he was in no position to do. He had never had a regular job. He and Shila were living with his mom and things were tight.

"I've never been the type to rob and hustle so my back was definitely against the wall," he said. "Look, I live in the ghetto and all you see is guns, drug dealers, credit card schemes, and any scam you can name. Risky quick fixes. I knew I wasn't capable of that. I've probably only ever been in one fight my whole life."

Now he was in a fight *for* his life. He made up his mind—he had to keep playing.

By the time the spring of 2002 rolled around, Al was back to playing every day. He knew AND 1 was beefing up the tour for the summer but felt the window might have closed on him.

"I really felt I missed my opportunity with AND 1," said Alimoe. "In the past I had been skeptical of the tour because I never really did tricks. People said I wouldn't be considered a basketball player if I played with them. That I'd be seen only as a trickster. But when I played serious I could throw it through your legs and snatch it back. That was just how I played. I hated the idea of people looking at me as anything but a serious ballplayer. I never wanted to be known as a trickball player."

Around midsummer, Al was once again invited to play in the New York stop of the Mix Tape Tour. The opposing team featured his boyhood friend God Shamgod, Lonnie "Prime Objective" Harrell, and Troy "Escalade" Jackson. This time Al was asked to suit up and start for AND 1. "It shocked me at first but I knew this was my chance to show what I could really do," Al recalled. With Al teamed up with Skip in the backcourt, AND 1 beat New York 118–115 and Alimoe played one of his best games in years.

Back at the team's hotel AND 1's Chris Hightower gave him the news that AND 1 wanted him to join the tour and finish out the summer. The next day he would leave for Seattle. It would be the farthest he had ever been from Harlem.

"Alimoe is one of the most down-to-earth individuals you can hope to meet," said street basketball oral historian Mike Ellis. "I've been watching him play since he was 13. If Alimoe isn't playing in a game then it's not real streetball."

"Earning money on the tour has given me the freedom to pursue other things," said Al. "I can go play in Europe or wherever because now I don't have to stay in New York and get a job to pay my bills. The tour has given me everything. It opened up my eyes to a life I never thought I was going to experience."

The 2002 tour ended in LA with Alimoe securing a permanent spot on the team. Back in Harlem his boys Mase, Cam, and Loon weren't surprised. His mother, Victoria, and his girlfriend, Shila, always knew he could do it. Now kids from other hoods around the country to lush suburban parks in middle America pretend to be the Black Widow as they break down their man or wrap the ball around their backs.

"At every stop all the kids scream 'Alimoe! Alimoe!'" said the Black Widow. "I can't describe the feeling that brings me, but I never forget to tell them that my first name is Tyron."

To see more of ALIMOE, check out:

- AND 1 Mix Tape Vol. 1
- AND 1 Mix Tape Vol. 6
- AND 1 Mix Tape Vol. 7
- Skip vs. Alimoe Battle Tape
- AND 1 Ball Access: The Mix Tape Tour
- Season 1 of ESPN's *StreetBall: The AND 1 Mix Tape Tour*
- Season 2 of ESPN's *StreetBall: The AND 1 Mix Tape Tour*

Troy Jackson

Escalade

TOUR DEBUT: 2003

Basketball is in his blood. Literally.

The same blood that flows through his veins flows through the NBA's all-time number-two assist man, his brother Mark Jackson. Since he had looked up to Mark for as long as he could remember, Troy almost had no choice but to get involved with basketball.

Growing up, Troy had heard the legend of Earl Manigault, Joe Hammond, and Pee Wee Kirkland from his three older brothers and his uncles. When Troy was 13, Mark, a junior and leading the nation in assists at St. Johns, took him to Rucker Park for the first time. He would not soon forget the experience.

"When we got there people were everywhere," said Escalade. "They hung from trees, stood on cars, and sat on each other's shoulders just to get a glimpse. The buzz around the park was unbelievable."

As the Jacksons made their way through the throng of people to the court, Troy spotted a man in his mid-thirties with a white full-length mink coat and a beautiful woman on each arm. When he took off the coat, the girls held it up by the shoulders so the guy could get dressed for the game.

"See that guy over there?" Mark asked. "That's Joe Hammond."

On the court Troy watched in amazement as Mark and his St. John teammates, Chris Mullin and Walter Berry, were hailed like kings every time they scored. Troy knew Mullin and Berry from the job Mark got him as a St. Johns ballboy. Mullin, who had just been named national player of the year, and Mark were roommates, so Troy often got to see the reaction the two got when they were out together. "I knew my brother was big but at the Rucker he was king," said Troy. "It was just incredible."

But before Troy saw his brother as a basketball star, he saw him as a brother. Mark would talk to his brother about the dangers of the streets. He didn't make a big deal of it, because by the time most kids are old enough to dribble they know how things can go down on the streets. But all the warning in the world can't prevent somebody from being an innocent bystander.

One summer night in 1991, Mark was on his way from his home in Jersey to pick up his brother and his best friend, Dave Snowden. They were waiting for Mark outside the Jacksons' home in Queens when several men began arguing down the block. The next thing they knew shots rang out, shattering the tranquillity of the tiny St. Albans block.

Dave and Troy took off running, but Troy turned around when he realized Dave wasn't following him. He was lying face down, having been shot in the spine. Dave lost the use of his legs.

"Dave was like part of our family," said Troy. "That night just made me appreciate life and my loved ones more."

In New York City basketball is about pride; about which borough is best. Hip-hop was born when Kangol-wearing rappers got on the mike and claimed that their own borough produced the best MCs. On the asphalt court of the city, the debate rages endlessly over which borough produces the illest ballers. Though Harlem is part of Manhattan, the abundance of home-grown talent reconfigures basketball geography and gives Harlem the right to rep itself as the sixth borough.

One Saturday morning in the summer of 1991, Escalade was

sleeping late when someone burst into his room and woke him, saying that he was urgently needed to play in a Harlem versus Queens streetball game. The winner would have bragging rights at least for the summer, but to raise the stakes, local high rollers put $10,000 on the game.

Lade got dressed and hurried uptown to the King Towers Projects to a local park called the King Dome at 116th and Lenox. Since he was well traveled in New York hoop circles he knew most of the faces on the Harlem squad. They were all there and they all could ball. The game was a physical affair, every shot challenged. Ball tricks were few and far between. Point guards were picked up at three-quarter court and each team sent three to the glass.

It seemed everyone brought his A game. But there was one kid who was on another level that day. Future AND 1 Mix Tape star Alimoe, aka the Black Widow, poured in 38 points while routinely taking the Queens players off the dribble and knocking down impossible shots from all over the court.

"Alimoe was killing us that day," said Escalade. "That's when I knew that cat was for real."

With two minutes to go in the game the score was knotted at 98. "Guys argued every single call in the last two minutes," remembered Escalade. "I've never seen people argue so much. Every time you even looked at someone a foul was called. Nobody wanted to pay out all that money if they lost."

In the end, the chance at 10 Gs wasn't as strong as the thought of losing so much money, and the players ultimately decide to end the game tied at 98.

When Troy graduated from junior high, Mark, who had just finished his second season with the Knicks, was asked to come speak to the kids. After the graduation ceremony, Troy's mother snapped a photo of her two sons together. After the film was developed, everyone realized for the first time that Troy was taller than Mark. (Mrs. Jackson still displays the picture in her living room.)

Escalade had always planned on hoop stardom. The adoration Mark received was something he thought he could get used to. During Mark's rookie year with the Knicks, he and Troy shared an apartment in the Bronx. And since Troy went everywhere with Mark, the spoils of NBA celebrity were all around him. In 1989, Mark's one and only All-Star appearance, Troy was a ballboy for the Eastern Conference All-Stars. He ran errands and straightened up the lockers of players like Larry Bird and Michael Jordan. After the game all of the players signed a ball, and Patrick Ewing gave him his Adidas, which he still proudly displays to this day.

The thrills kept coming when Troy's favorite player sent him a handwritten letter just before he faced off against his brother one year. The letter was signed by Magic Johnson, the only player in NBA history to hand out more assists than his brother Mark. Troy remembered, "I loved Magic more than anything but when he was playing against Mark I hated him."

By his junior year, Jackson owned a mammoth 6-10 frame that carried 560 pounds. Hills East's football coaches tried relentlessly to recruit Jackson to the gridiron but he wouldn't budge. "I never gave it any thought," said Jackson. "We didn't have a big-time football program. Our field didn't even have grass."

After averaging 19 points, 12 rebounds, and 4 blocks, the heavily recruited heavy narrowed his college choices to Louisville, Seton Hall, Georgia Tech, Arkansas, and St. Johns. "Everyone automatically assumed that I'd go to St. Johns because Mark went there," said Jackson. "But the problem was that St. Johns thought that too. They barely went after me. I felt they really disrespected me by not trying to recruit me. They went after Felipe Lopez and Zendon Hamilton hard. To them, I was an afterthought."

After getting the cold shoulder from the Johnnies, Jackson headed for JUCO ball at George C. Wallace State Community College in Selma, Alabama, where he averaged 10 points and 5.5 rebounds while shooting 54 percent from the field.

In September 1995, Troy committed to Louisville, partly because of the zest with which Bronx native Louisville assistant coach Scotter McCray recruited Jackson. But there was another plus. After the 1994–95 season, Mark was traded by the Clippers to the Indiana Pacers. With only 109 miles separating the brothers, Troy could easily head to Indy to see his brother play.

Louisville proved to be the right choice. Head Coach Denny Crum diagrammed a freewheeling style and preached to his players that basketball should be fun. Crum was adamant that Jackson trim down if he wanted to see the floor. He entered Louisville at about 560 pounds and trimmed down to 350, his lowest weight in years, thanks to a closely monitored diet of turkey sandwiches, Caesar salads, and fruit.

He also stopped eating after eight o'clock and stayed after practice to run. ESPN's *Outside the Lines* featured Troy in a segment on athletes and weight loss titled, "The Weight Debate: Sports by the Pound." Troy's jersey size was listed as XXXXL and the Louisville media guide pointed out that "he's the tallest and heaviest player on the team."

Jackson's Cardinals made the NCAA tournament in each of his four seasons, advancing to the Elite Eight in 1997 and the Sweet Sixteen the following year.

The morning of Louisville's Elite Eight matchup with North Carolina, Troy and his teammates were fitted for Final Four rings.

It proved to be premature. After staying within a few points of the Antawn Jamison/Vince Carter/Shammond Williams three-headed monster, a succession of back-door alley-oops by Carter sealed the Cards' fate.

The finish was disappointing but not enough to dampen Jackson's spirits. After all, he had played in great halls he'd seen on TV such as Freedom Hall, Rupp Arena, and UCLA's Pauley Pavilion.

"College was the best time of my life," said Jackson. "I have nothing but fond memories of Coach Crum, Freedom Hall, and Louisville. They love their basketball just as much as New Yorkers. Every night we'd be 20,000 strong in Freedom Hall. We were the only game in town."

Indeed, in a local poll, Jackson was voted one of the 20 most-loved University of Louisville athletes of all time, right alongside such luminaries as Darrell Griffith and Johnny Unitas. "Even to this day the love I get when I go back to Louisville is amazing," said Jackson.

"He has unbelievable heart and the talent to match," Mark said. "There's always been a lot of pressure on him because his brother is in the NBA. People have always said he should make it, too. But the NBA is not for everybody and I always felt in my heart that Troy would be successful at whatever he wanted to do."

In 2000, without any other prospects, Jackson took up with the legendary Harlem Globetrotters. But he quickly realized that the choreo- graphed game that was the signature of the Trotters did not mesh well with his com- petitive nature. He had, after all, played in four NCAA tournaments. "My time with the Globetrotters was the low point in my career," remembered Escalade. "I mean, no disrespect to them, but it wasn't basketball. It was more like a stage play. We were actors being told our cues. Being told our lines. Everything was scripted and to me that just wasn't what I was looking for.

"When they wanted me to do a certain move they would click the lights. Other times there were hand signals or key words. It was a paycheck but I made up my mind that I didn't want to be a part of this and I left. And I knew I wasn't coming back."

Skip had always been on his friend about joining the Mix Tape Tour, but Escalade staunchly resisted. "I always considered myself a serious basketball player, someone legit. I wanted competition and I didn't think I could get it by playing AND 1's style of bas- ketball. My experience with the Globetrotters made me even more wary. I didn't want somebody telling me when I could make a move, or worse, the defender letting me make a move without trying to stop me."

After the New York stop of the 2002 Mix Tape Tour, Skip finally convinced his friend of 20 years to join. On that day Troy played for the New York team, which lost 118–115, but his bone-crushing dunk over High Octane had AND 1 pleading with him to join. The decision changed his life.

Since Louisville, he had been toiling in basketball's underbelly. His hoopological clock was ticking. While NBA stardom slipped from his grasp, Escalade has become a tour favorite thanks to his showmanship, girth, and good-natured attitude.

"The fans love Es because of his personality," said Shane The Dribbling Machine. "When they see him on the court they can't help but to cheer for him."

And he's more famous than he could ever have been as a career sub in the NBA. "The 2003 tour was my first and it blew my mind," says Escalade. "We're like rock stars out here. People just go crazy for us when we roll into town. I never thought I would get this kind of reaction from people through basketball without making it to the NBA."

But after years of seeing Mark gracefully handle fame, Troy has handled his new spotlight with ease. With a brother like Jax, you can't exactly get a big head.

"I've been in this business for 20 years and Mark has been my best friend every step of the way," said Troy. "He's always had advice for me and treats me like a brother no matter how success-ful he ever became. I can't say enough about how close we are." He's heavy, but he's still my brother.

But Mark can still surprise him after all these years. In December 2003, Troy was visiting Mark's home in Utah when he saw that his older brother had all of the episodes of *StreetBall* saved on his TiVo. "He didn't even tell me," said Troy. "That's what made me feel good."

After nearly two decades of people constantly asking Troy about his more famous brother, the tables are finally starting to turn. Almost everywhere Mark goes people want to know what it's like to be the brother "of that big guy on the AND 1 Mix Tape Tour."

Once the two were at a cell-phone store at the Garden State

Plaza not far from Mark's New Jersey home when a fan asked Mark if it was okay to take a picture with Escalade and not *him*. Mark smiled, shook his head in amazement, and agreed. The little brother who cast such a big shadow was finally out of his.

"Sometimes I can't believe it," says Escalade. "There's not a day that goes by that I don't get recognized. It's just unbelievable."

To see more of ESCALADE, check out:

- AND 1 Mix Tape Vol. 7
- AND 1 Ball Access: The Mix Tape Tour
- Season 1 of ESPN's *StreetBall: The AND 1 Mix Tape Tour*
- Season 2 of ESPN's *StreetBall: The AND 1 Mix Tape Tour*

Aaron Owens
AO
TOUR DEBUT: 2000

As an undersized teammate of Rasheed Wallace and Aaron McKie at Philly's Simon Gratz High, Aaron Owens's career best was eight points. In his junior season he backed up former Maryland point guard Terrell Stokes. AO scored just eight points all season. Yes, *season*.

Now, depending on who you ask, AO is more popular than his former teammates now in the NBA. His slick moves and trademark headwrap are more identifiable with young hoop fans than Rasheed's techs or McKie's whatever he's known for.

But back in the early nineties, Wallace and McKie, who went on to sparkling college careers at North Carolina and Temple, respectively, were the pride of Philadelphia and Simon Gratz. Aaron was a five-seven third-string practice player whom reporters never talked to and who never saw an ounce of high-school glory.

Sheed got dozens of letters every day that he would hand out to friends as if they were Christmas cards.

Every team needs a twelfth man, and instead of transferring to another school, where he could have started, he stayed with Gratz and its top-shelf basketball pedigree. Head coach Brian Ellerbee always stressed making something out of oneself outside basketball.

"I'm really proud of Aaron," Ellerbee, now an assistant at Temple, told the *Philadelphia Inquirer* in 2003. "He's doing very well. He was a real kid. Everybody loved him at Gratz. He was a

very popular guy and a good student too. It's just that he played when we had two national championship teams. Aaron didn't weigh much more than 100 pounds. He was very frail. But he could play the game. He had some skills. He developed after high school."

He grew up in North Philly on 24th and Somerset in the heart of one of the toughest areas of the city. But all the kid ever wanted to do was play ball. And you couldn't name a court around the city where he didn't know every crack in the asphalt—Connie Mack court at 22nd at Lehigh, Simons Playground, 16th and Susquehanna, Walnut Lane and Woolston Street, Myers Recreation Center, 58th and Kingsessing, Sherwood Recreation Center, 56th and Christian streets, 30th and Wharton streets, and 52nd and Parkside Avenue.

North Philly is AO's home. But it's also home to some memories he would rather shake. He never knew his dad. And what he knew of his biological mother, Jeanette Owens, he wanted to forget. Not that he doesn't love moms—"I see her almost every day, she's where I got my sense of humor from," said AO—it's just that her battle with substance abuse was hard on nine-year-old Aaron.

"She's always my mom, but the drinking had her. It got to the point I just stopped crying," AO said.

As a youngster he was involved in the church and met a woman named Brenda Tucker. On a church trip to Disney World the two bonded and AO asked her if he could move in. From that day on Tucker has raised AO as one of her own children.

After Gratz he played in the Sonny Hill League, a competitive semipro league home to Philly's best summer run. When he wasn't playing he kicked around North Philly trying to keep his nose clean. "It's real easy to fall into doing dumb stuff," said AO. This is how he spent the first two years after graduation.

In the summer of 1995, AO was introduced to the athletic director at Lackawanna Community College in Scranton, Pennsylvania, who wanted to see what AO had. He took AO to a local park in Scranton to run with the locals. The next day he called AO back in Philly to offer him a scholarship. A few weeks later he saw 24th and Somerset fade out in the rearview mirror as he headed for Scranton, a town better known for high-school football powerhouses and steel mills than for its junior colleges.

He played decently but Lackawanna turned out to be a pit stop. He needed a new beginning. In the summer after his freshman year, through a 76ers scout, he met Bob Schermahorn, the head coach at Riverside Community College in Riverside, California. He was offered a scholarship and decided to jumpstart his life by heading out west.

His Riverside experience was far from Gratz. There, AO was the star, quickly settling in and winning the starting point guard role. He scraped together enough for a one-way ticket and was gone again. To become eligible under California's JUCO requirements he ended up taking classes from 7:30 in the morning to 4:30 each day in the summer of 1996. He stayed with a surrogate family arranged by the team.

"I was out there by myself," remembered Owens. "I didn't know anybody, but I knew this is what I had to do."

If I don't make it, I can live with that. I'm having fun and getting paid to play ball. There are a lot of people who can't say that.

He had hoped to lead Riverside to the California junior college state finals, but his dreams were dashed on March 5, 1997, when Riverside was beaten by Antelope Valley 104–83. AO scored 29 points for the Tigers, who finished the regular season 22–13. In one season at Riverside he averaged 14.3 points and 8.1 assists and was named first team All Orange Empire conference and honorable mention all state.

He got looks from D1 schools such as Long Beach State, Cal State Fullerton, and Cal State Bakersfield. But Wyoming was the only school talking scholarship. A few weeks later, after consulting his mother, AO signed a letter of intent to play at Division II powerhouse Fort Hays State where he decided he would get more run.

Besides, at Fort Hays he knew his chances of winning a championship were strong. Just two years before they had gone 34–0 and won the NCAA Division II title. He liked the idea of playing for head coach Gary Garner, who had turned Hays into a national power. But two weeks after he signed his letter of intent, Garner took a job at Southwest Missouri State.

While at FHSU, AO rang up 15.5 points and 5.1 assists per game but didn't get along with the new coach, Mark Johnson. "He thought he was Bobby Knight but I wasn't trying to hear that," said AO. He inquired about D2 powerhouse Kentucky Wesleyan. The school sent him a brochure that detailed its sprawling campus, with a student body of 8,000.

"When I went there on my recruiting visit I saw they had like one building," AO said. "I left immediately."

He then received a scholarship offer from Henderson State in Arkadelphia, Arkansas, which had a nationally ranked program. But his early Henderson experiences weren't what he had hoped for. Late that summer he tore his meniscus and was forced to sit out fall workouts. Add to that the fact that he was the only East Coast player on the team, and no one identified with his peculiar fashion. "They had never seen anybody wear shorts and Timberlands before," he said. "They were looking at me like I was crazy."

One weekend AO extended an invitation to his teammates to go see *Rush Hour*, which had just been released. His boys declined, saying they had other plans. The next morning at the gym everyone was talking about how funny Chris Tucker was in the movie. When AO walked in everyone got quiet.

"After that I felt alienated," said AO. "To me they were petty."

But shortly after he returned to the court and a 4–6 team, he won over his teammates by orchestrating workouts over Christmas break. Soon after, the players gelled and the team won 19 of its next 20 heading into the D2 tournament. They advanced to the Elite Eight. The eventual champion? Kentucky Wesleyan.

After his eligibility had run out, he was back with Mom, back on 24th and Somerset in North Philly, back with his boys JO and Nate, back playing pickup around the way. Six months later he got invited to a New York versus Philly pickup game at Temple. The game featured a baller named Ronald "Flip" Murray, who was sitting out a year at Philadelphia CC to get his grades in order so he could apply to Shaw University in North Carolina. (Three years later Flip made a huge splash with the Seattle Supersonics, averaging 13 points a game, and was considered one of the surprise players of the decade.)

But there was something about AO that caught the eye of former AND 1 marketing director Jeff Roth, who was scouting for talented streetball players to take on a nationwide tour.

"His energy was infectious," said Roth. "Plus he had the type of skills we were looking for."

He saw how the crowd responded to AO's tricks, such as going between an opponent's legs—with his entire body, and bouncing the ball off defenders' foreheads. Roth immediately signed him to the original 2000 Mix Tape Tour, which hit three cities, LA, Chicago, and Atlanta.

When the tour ended, he played for Maccabi Karniel in Israel's top division, where he averaged 17.1 points per game

before leaving with two weeks left in the season when the team was holding out on his paper.

"I couldn't deal with not getting paid," said AO. "I mean, I did the work, so you can't not pay me. I loved playing basketball but I had to make a living to feed my daughter."

The words ring like those of Biggie Smalls at the beginning of "Juicy." But unlike B.I.G., AO saw no way out on the streets. They were a place that you didn't come back from.

But now he was an official Mix Tape baller, so he didn't have to worry about that. But just so he would never forget the block, he and his boys had the street sign at the intersection of 24th and Somerset tattooed on the inside of his right forearm.

"I accept the fact that I may never play in the NBA," said AO, "but I play rec ball for a living. How great is that?" And he knows who he has to thank. "Do I owe Skip?" he asks. "Yes, sir."

AO still dreams about basketball's holy grail—the league. "I'm still trying to get there," he said. "But if I don't make it I can live with that. I'm having fun and getting paid to play ball. There are a lot of people who can't say that."

He got closer than most when he helped the Mobile Revelers of the NBDL win the championship in the 2002–03 season. He had highs of 18 points, 9 assists, 6 steals. But being recognized as one of the best streetballers in the country has been more than he ever expected.

"People are always asking for my autograph, calling my name, or trying to get pictures with me," said AO. "That just gives me a good feeling. To know that I'm reaching so many people because of basketball. That's always something I wanted to do but it didn't always look like that was going to be a possibility. Not when I was sitting at the end of Gratz's bench dreaming about being a star."

Not everybody can be that twelfth man. And not everybody can be AO.

To see more of AO, check out:

- AND 1 Mix Tape Vol. 3
- AND 1 Mix Tape Vol. 4
- AND 1 Mix Tape Vol. 5
- AND 1 Mix Tape Vol. 6
- AND 1 Mix Tape Vol. 7
- AND 1 Ball Access: The Mix Tape Tour
- Season 1 of ESPN's *StreetBall: The AND 1 Mix Tape Tour*
- Season 2 of ESPN's *StreetBall: The AND 1 Mix Tape Tour*

Philip Champion
Hot Sauce

TOUR DEBUT: 2000

If you heard the S word you knew you were done. "Sauce!" Philip Champion would call out as he let fly jumpers from deep. During the mid-nineties at Atlanta's Run-n-Shoot, the 24-hour hoop gym, you were more likely to catch him shooting from deep than tossing some kid a Boomerang. "I've always had flash to my game but back then I concentrated more on real basketball," he said.

So every time he released a jumper he shouted, "Sauce." He would say it so much that the tag line began to precede him. Other ballers started calling him Sauce when he walked into the gym. "There goes that dude Sauce," they would say. When he

missed, kids began to mock him by calling him Tomato Sauce or some other variation. But he was on more often than not, and the nickname eventually morphed into Hot Sauce. Philip Champion ran with it. Up to that point, most people from his neighborhood in Columbus, 45 minutes outside Hotlanta, knew him as Phil the Thrill.

But at the Run-n-Shoot he was simply Hot Sauce. When he did a move dudes would go back to their hoods and tell people about a kid named Hot Sauce with crazy moves no one had ever seen before. The name just rolled off the tongue a lot smoother than Phil the Thrill.

"That's when my name took over," said Sauce. "People wanted to know me and see me play just because of my name. People just like saying it because it's so catchy."

He calls the Dirty South home but Sauce came into this world by way of Fort Campbell, Kentucky. His father, Emmanuel, and his mother, Velda, split up when the boy was young. Mom went to live in Jacksonville, Florida, while Pops landed in Columbus. For much of his early years he spent time going back and forth between the two cities.

Wherever he was, he always had a basketball in his hands. "All I wanted to do was play ball," he said. "I didn't feel right if I wasn't dribbling. If I didn't have a ball I would go in other people's yards and steal their balls."

When his mother sent him to the store for milk, he dribbled his way there. Sometimes he would get distracted if he dribbled by one of the neighborhood courts. At the court behind his apartment building there would sometimes be a hundred kids gathered around the fence waiting for next. Three hours later he would arrive home with the milk. Usually warm.

In the ninth grade he entered Sandlewood High School in Jacksonville but didn't even get the chance to go out for the team. His father, a sergeant in the army, was stationed in Germany and he brought Philip to live with him. There he spent the rest of his high-school days on an army base playing ball with army kids and picking up a little German here and there. (Nowadays all he can say in German is "chocolate" and "good morning.")

In 1994, after he graduated high school, he returned to the States and continued to play ball. He'd play in pickup games whenever he could or just dribble around the neighborhood when he had time—which was almost always.

But he needed to pull down some bread, so between games he decided to pick up a trade and enrolled in the Brunswick Job Center. He took classes in the culinary arts and welding. But when classes broke for lunch it was usually the last time the instructors saw Sauce that day. "I would just head straight to a basketball court and look for a game," said Sauce. "Usually I would end up staying for hours. I did that almost every day and eventually they just kicked me out of the school."

At Brunswick, he met fellow student Morris Vaughn, who first began to take him to the Run-n-Shoot. He would hit the gym and after five or six hours of ball, go upstairs to an exercise room that had mirrors from floor to ceiling along one of the walls. There, staring at his reflection, he would dribble for hours, creating move after move. The guy had handle like someone who slept in a gym. Well, that's because he did.

Sometimes he couldn't afford the daily fee to play at the gym, and he and Morris would have to sneak in. Instead of risking sneaking in two days in a row, Sauce would sometimes just spend the night in the upstairs exercise room. He would roll out the tumbling mats and go to sleep with the basketball as his pillow.

In the morning he would wake up and make it seem as if he had just arrived. "It's crazy when you think about it," said Sauce. "I went from having to sneak in to getting a free lifetime VIP pass."

Ballers from Decatur to Marietta would see his moves and take them back to their own hoods. Before long word had spread throughout the Dirty about a skinny kid who had more moves than he knew what to do with.

But with trade school not working out, Sauce began a string of odd jobs that would always take a backseat to basketball. First there was the job at Wendy's. "All I wanted to do was sit in the back and talk about basketball," Sauce said. Often he'd be late because he'd stop for a game on the way to work. "I'd be wearing my Wendy's uniform just clowning people."

The Wendy's gig didn't last long. Soon after that Sauce got a job selling magazine subscriptions door-to-door. When people refused to buy, Sauce made them a deal: Play me one-on-one. You win, I leave. I win, you buy. People got suckered in because at 140 pounds, Sauce wasn't very imposing. He sold more than a few subscriptions that way. Jobs washing dishes at Red Lobster and working night security followed. But they were always secondary to basketball.

He didn't even watch hoops on TV because he was too busy playing. The boy never had NBA aspirations either. "I just wanted to play," he said. "That's all I cared about." Back then getting paid to play streetball wasn't even an option. But that hardly mattered.

By 1999, Sauce had lost interest in odd jobs and fast food joints and started running with the wrong crowd. "He would get into petty stuff that he had no business doing," said Mark Edwards, a Georgia College graduate who became Sauce's business manager. In the summer of 2000, his petty crime landed him in jail for a year. He then struck a deal with the judge that would free him if he paid a $755 fine.

Sauce had no money and no one else to bail him out when Edwards sprung him loose. While Sauce was locked down, Edwards, who had contacts at AND 1 from his days as a shoe store manager, promised the company he could deliver them the best streetballer around when he heard they were starting a street team. The problem was he couldn't find Sauce. All he knew was that Sauce had recently stopped showing up at the Run-n-Shoot.

Edwards got word that he had been locked up and scoured local jails until he found Sauce. "I looked all over the place and they kept telling me he had been moved," said Edwards. When Sauce got out he hopped a plane three days later to play sight unseen in the AND 1 game in California in July 2000, the first year of the Mix Tape Tour.

He was electrifying. His moves, which had only been known to those at the Run-n-Shoot, made him a cinch to sign with AND 1. Sauce had seen the first Mix Tape featuring Skip and was enthralled that people in other parts of the country played with similar flair.

In no time he became the main attraction on tour. Everyone

clamored for his crossovers and ball tricks. Kids would soon study him on Mix Tape Vols. 3 and 4 the way they studied Skip on Vol. 1. But it would not be without a price.

"The way they did the Mix Tapes and the TV shows made it look like I was all about moves," said Sauce. "As a result, every city I go to people just want me to break someone down. Everybody I face is a matchup with an isolation. Why can't we play back and forth? They always want to slow the game down to see me do a trick. I'm at the point in my career where I want to concentrate on my real game. I don't like people thinking I'm just a trickballer. There is a lot of pressure on me to perform but when you do the same move city after city, and the defense knows what you're going to do, it gets tough to be that guy who has to constantly entertain."

Unlike most fans, Sauce knows the moves (he doesn't think of them as tricks) are just for show. "You can't do the Flintstones shuffle in a real game. You're not going to Sauce2K anybody who's playing real defense. Most people are just afraid to get embarrassed trying to steal the ball from you and play zombie defense," he said. "The only way you can drop somebody in a game is with a regular crossover. It's a surprise move that you do in the flow of a real game. That's what I want to concentrate on.

"When you break down what basketball is all about, moves are what you use to free yourself for a shot. But no one ever cares if I shoot or even make the shot. They just want to see the moves and somebody get shook."

Regardless, on the tour, his moves have made him the most popular streetball player in the world (now that Skip's in the NBA). He's appeared in advertising campaigns from Mountain Dew Code Red to Lays potato chips. He's also had cameos in videos by Chingy and Lil' Bow Wow.

Sauce has since expanded his streetball empire by headlining his own tour in the off-season, which tries to find up-and-coming streetball talent.

"All Sauce has ever cared about is basketball," said Edwards. "I mean sometimes he wouldn't eat because he was out playing. I've never seen a person on any level who has a pure love for the game the way Sauce does."

"Everybody can dribble," said Sauce. "Everybody's got crossovers and can go between the legs, that stuff is universal. But few people can invent tricks. When I go on tour everybody's doing my moves. But I got a million signature moves. More signatures than the Constitution. Now it's time for me to sit back, watch, and take moves from everybody else."

To see more of HOT SAUCE, check out:

- AND 1 Mix Tape Vol. 3
- AND 1 Mix Tape Vol. 4
- AND 1 Mix Tape Vol. 5
- AND 1 Mix Tape Vol. 6
- AND 1 Mix Tape Vol. 7
- AND 1 Ball Access: The Mix Tape Tour
- Season 1 of ESPN's *StreetBall: The AND 1 Mix Tape Tour*
- Season 2 of ESPN's *StreetBall: The AND 1 Mix Tape Tour*

Lonnie Harrell
Prime Objective
TOUR DEBUT: 2003

On a muggy August morning in Washington, D.C., Lonnie Harrell sat on a rickety folding chair smack in the middle of the asphalt courts outside Georgetown's McDonough Arena. He sat perfectly still with the arms he borrowed from Jar Jar Binks resting in his lap. It's 96 degrees. "Man it ain't even eleven o'clock yet," he said. The unforgiving sun doesn't care for makeshift statues, sending beads of sweat drag racing down the L-Train tattoo on his left biceps. The year was 1999 and Lonnie was 26. This place, McDonough, used to be his home. The Washington, D.C., native was a teammate of Alonzo Mourning and Dikembe Mutombo on Georgetown's 1991–92 season Sweet Sixteen squad.

But that's not why this was his home. For the last 23 years G-Town's campus gym has been home to the James "Jabbo" Kenner League, the capital city's most storied run. It was here that AI played his first organized basketball after he was let out of prison in 1994. Grant Hill and Dike arrived late and had to stand five rows deep. (AI dropped 40.) It was here that Greg Jones, long believed to be the inventor of Iverson's "DC" crossover, once scored 62 against a team of NBA pros.

But it was Lonnie's legend that loomed the largest. At six-seven, with a point guard's mentality and handle, Harrell's feathery no-looks, sleight of hand, and behind-the-back fakes kept fans entertained for more than 10 summers. "I could always score," says Harrell, "but my game was always about setting people up.

97

In the Kenner, competition
was more important than
style, but there has always
been creativity to my game."
In 1996, Lonnie was the
last man cut by the
Orlando Magic, thanks to
a bum ankle. The experi-
ence was positive in that
he became a close friend
of the first team All-NBA
star Penny Hardaway.
From there it was back to
Washington. He then
floated around low-budget pro teams like the
Washington Generals, collecting free shoes, pulling paychecks of
about $300 a week, wondering if he would ever make a living
from the game he loved.

Of all his minor-league experiences none was worse than the
Washington Congressionals. In summer 1999, Harrell joined the
second-year USBL franchise in what seemed a promising situation. After all, the team's point guard was current Knick Moochie
Norris, whom Lonnie had known for over 10 years.

Halfway into the season the Congressionals were riding a 15-
game losing streak. They had to routinely forfeit because man-
agement could not secure a gym for its home games. Once
Moochie's car got a flat and he missed a game in New Jersey.
Head coach Mike McCleese abandoned the team eight games into
the season. He said he'd never been paid and took the team's uniforms with him when he left.

Harrell himself was also having money problems. The team
only gave him one of his paychecks, which bounced when he
tried to cash it.

It was clear Lonnie needed a new scene. He made tracks up

north to New York to test his game against some of the best streetballers around. He became a regular at the Entertainer's league at Rucker Park, where Duke Tango gave him the moniker Prime Objective, because his first and only goal was to destroy his opponent.

In summer 2000, the L-Train's credibility got a huge boost when he teamed with Vince Carter for a game at the Gauchos gym in New York. Air Canada threw down several alley-oops that defied logic and sent fans pouring hysterically onto the court. The setup man? Prime Objective.

"It's great when you play with someone like that," said Prime. "All you have to do is put it up there and he'll go get it."

Lonnie decided to leave Congress Park and D.C. behind and move to New York full-time. After two years he had built his legend in the Big Apple as if he had lived there all his life. But he was 28 and his window to the league was closing. He had to make a move. In October 2001 he got a break. He was invited to the New Jersey Nets preseason camp and tested his skills in scrimmages against Jason Kidd. After three days of shooting the ball well, he was called into Coach Byron Scott's office. Scott told him to keep working on his game but that "the team was going in another direction." He was cut.

Like just about every streetballer you can find, Harrell dreams of making it to the proverbial next level. But there's a problem. He feels the league won't give him the fair shot he deserves because of his streetball reputation. Thus, his addition to AND 1's Mix Tape team has become a blessing and a curse. On the one hand, he's getting the opportunity to play the game he loves. On the other, his Mix Tape runs enforce his streetballer rep.

"The second I dribble through my legs at a tryout," says Harrell "scouts are going to say, 'That's the street in him.'"

The Mix Tape Tour allows him to support himself financially, which paves the way for him to pursue lower-paying mainstream opportunities, jobs that could lead directly to the league.

Two weeks after the Nets tryout, Lonnie caught a plane to the Suwanee Sports Academy in Suwanee, Georgia, site of the NBDL's inaugural training camp. Players, most of them former midlevel D1 stars, wearing jerseys numbering in the hundreds, waited in a gym with five full courts like nervous children on the first day of elementary school. There was one player who wasn't nervous at all. Lonnie calmly hoisted rainbow threes from halfcourt with a toothy grin.

"I'm not worried about anything," he said. "This is basketball and basketball is my life." During the orientation that followed the players had to fill out a questionnaire. The first question: List

four things that cause
you stress. In big, block
uppercase letters Lonnie
wrote "NOT BEING IN
THE LEAGUE." He left the
rest of the lines blank.

The L-Train played
well enough to be drafted
number eight overall
by the Huntsville
Flight and finished his
first season with averages
of 14 points and 4 assists.

Harrell is the NBDL career
leader in games played (115)
and started (106). He spent the first three years with the Flight,
but at 31 decided to leave the NBDL behind in 2004. "They know
who they want to call up anyway," he said.

During his Flight time, PO continued to return to New York in
the summers, and after a strong performance against the AND 1
team at Riverbank Park in 2002, he was asked to become a full-
time tour member.

His call is likely never to come, but with the AND 1 Mix Tape
Tour, the Prime Objective just may have found his calling.

To see more of PRIME OBJECTIVE, check out:

- AND 1 Mix Tape Vol. 7
- AND 1 Ball Access: The Mix Tape Tour
- Season 1 of ESPN's *StreetBall: The AND 1 Mix Tape Tour*
- Season 2 of ESPN's *StreetBall: The AND 1 Mix Tape Tour*

Shane Woney

Shane the Dribbling Machine

TOUR DEBUT: 2000

Like most streetballers, Shane Woney's fascination with the game started young, and, in his case, quite by accident, when he tagged along with his stepfather to one of his men's league games when he was nine years old. His stepfather worked on Wall Street for the firm Dean Witter, which sponsored a team for its employees after hours. During halftime of one of the games Shane took the ball and began shooting at one of the baskets.

"I made like five or six shots in a row when everybody started to look up at me," recalled Shane. The coach of a local pee wee team was at the gym that night and asked Shane's stepfather if Shane could play for his Madison Square Broncos.

Despite the fact that the Broncos featured players who were a couple of years older than Shane, he made a trip to New Jersey to play in his first game the following week.

"I wasn't even close to being the best one on the team, but I got a good feeling when some of the older guys gave me compliments," said Shane.

His stepfather took his boy not only to his basketball games but also to company softball and touch football outings. Whether it was being a batboy or waterboy, Shane found a way to chip in. But it was basketball that best kept Shane's attention.

"He taught me so much about the game and how to approach it," said Shane. "I'd see how aggressive he was and how serious

he took it and I'd want to be just like that. He was a hacker and got into fights, so he had to have a toughness about him every time he played."

Shane picked up his stepfather's aggressive approach but had the knack for a more finesse-oriented game. "Dribbling was always something I could do, so I knew I wanted to exploit that," Woney offered.

In his early teens, Shane became a regular at all of the local hot spots. Rucker Park, Dyckman, 112th, Valley, Gun Hill, and up in Mt. Vernon were some of the spots Shane would grab five and run till dark. But Sousa Park in the Bronx was where he learned how to drop his defender at the foul line with a crossover, finish at the rim, and pick up the and one time and time again. "Sousa Park was home to me," he said, "that's where I got my game from. If you couldn't play you knew not to show up."

The fast-paced style at Sousa prepared him to make the junior-high team at PS 142. Over the course of his seventh- and eighth-grade years, Shane's teams went 36–0 and were so dominant they would often schedule high-school JV teams. When 142 played Clinton High's junior varsity, Clinton's coach asked Shane to play for him as a freshman. But when he failed to make Clinton's varsity, he was relegated to its frighteningly awful JV team.

"The JV was so sorry I had to play center," recalled Shane, "and I was five-eight!"

Going against taller, less skilled players every night, he averaged over 30 points per game. But after the season Shane's class attendance was spotty and his parents transferred him to the more rigid Faleshian High School in New Rochelle, New York. This meant he would face tougher competiton in New York's Catholic High School Athletic Association. It also meant his days playing center were over.

In his sophomore season he teamed with future NBA prospect 6-10 Eric Mobley. Woney averaged 19 points, 10 assists, and 6 steals, but New Rochelle was eliminated in the second round of

the CHSAA playoffs. By the time his junior year rolled around, his name had begun to get around New York basketball circles as that of someone to keep your eye on. In 1989, the man everybody was talking about was Kenny Anderson of Archbischop Malloy, the best prep player in the country. Shane put up respectable numbers but got little attention.

The summer following his junior year he teamed up with Kentucky-bound Jamal Mashburn and ran roughshod over other local AAU clubs. At the B/C All-Star camp, a high-profile summer camp in Pennsylvania, Woney played well enough to earn his way into the camp's Top 20 all-star game. The other key event that summer was the ouster of his high-school coach. The new staff brought in several new players at almost every position, and Shane was left virtually out of the rotation.

"I made it to the second preseason scrimmage and hardly even played," he said. "After that I just quit."

To keep his game shape during his senior year, Shane played in night leagues and pickup spots throughout the city. By spring he hadn't received any attention from major college programs

and was lightly recruited. In May 1990, after his senior year, he took a recruiting visit to Champlain College, a junior college in Vermont. Norman Marbury, older brother of Knicks guard Stephon Marbury, happened to make a visit to the school on the same weekend. Neither player decided to enroll, but several weeks later Woney enrolled at Westchester College, a junior college about 30 minutes away from his Bronx home.

In his freshman year, he adjusted to college life quickly and earned a role as the squad's starting point guard. To motivate his players, Shane's coach had the habit of hyping the opposing team's players by saying there was no way they could be guarded. One such player was a San Jacinto's All-America sophomore point guard Sam Cassell, whom Westchester aced in a tournament in Pensacola, Florida, in 1991.

"Coach told us that he had the handle of Kenny Anderson and the jumpshot of Chris Jackson," remembered Woney. "We thought he was going to be the best thing we'd ever seen."

But in the first half Cassell was the kid who couldn't shoot straight, tallying just four points. "I was like, this dude is nobody," said Woney. But in the second half the nobody became somebody. Cassell caught fire, dropping one three after another. He finished with 38 points. "All you heard was 'Sam Cassell for three! Sam Cassell for three!'" said Shane. "Coach wasn't lying about him. We couldn't do nothing with him in the second half."

Aside from Cassell's thrashing, Shane had no problem leading Westchester to a number-eight national ranking and a trip to the junior college nationals in Hudson, Kansas, in 1991.

"When I look back to JC ball, I really consider that some of the best moments I've had in my life," said Woney.

After his sophomore year, Shane returned home to the Bronx without garnering attention from any four-year schools. More important, he had someone to look after—his infant son. His son put life in perspective, and now Shane had to figure out how he was going to provide. He played in several night leagues without finding a job until he heard about a minor-league team based in Springfield, Massachusetts, called the Harlem Rockets.

By every account the Rockets were a low-budget, shoestring operation. Houston this wasn't. The team traveled from the Northeast to the South playing in low-rent, backwoods facilities with uninterested crowds and crude accommodations.

"We played in towns so small you can't find them on the map," said Shane. "I'm not even sure they all had names."

The Rockets played in decrepit gyms, some of them not much more than glorified barns. They traveled in unreliable vans that would often break down. Sometimes they slept in the gyms they were to play in the next night. Other times it was $49-a-night motels. In some stops in the Deep South he would talk to kids after the game who had never seen a black person before they met Shane. One gym they played in had pictures of the KKK on the wall. "The other team's mascot was a Klansman," said Woney. "That's when I knew I had to get out of there."

But the Rockets paid $100 a game. Not much, but when he couldn't find work in New York he had to take what he could to feed his son. From September to May the team would play over a hundred games, which allowed Shane to send money home to his son.

This kind of basketball existence was a long way from the fun he used to have on hot summer nights at Sousa Park where he made up for his lack of size by dribbling circles around the locals. This kind of basketball lacked the passion he felt at Rucker Park. And face it, he missed his boys. The local streetball scene was where Shane met a lot of his closest friends, whom he still counts in his inner posse. At one summer run he met a high-flying banger named Waliyy Dixon from Linden, New Jersey. Waliyy was a couple of years younger, but the two bonded instantly.

One day one of Shane's boys came back to the projects after a summer-league game raving about how he got dunked on that day. Getting flushed on is something you want as few people to know about as possible. But homeboy was going around telling anybody who would listen, "I just got banged on by this dude from New Jersey about 16 years old. I never seen someone so young jump that high."

Shane began to put two and two together and later found out it was his boy Waliyy Dixon. "That's when I said I need to keep my eye on this guy," said Shane.

After a turbulent college career at Rutgers, he told Waliyy about the Harlem Rockets and he, along with Rucker legend Malloy "Future" Nesmith, joined Shane on the traveling minstrel show.

With Waliyy on board, at least he could handle the mind-numbing travel, the lack of recognition, and the frequent misadventures due to inclement weather. "Having my boy there made basketball fun again," said Shane, "but I knew that I couldn't do that forever."

In 1998, Shane left the Rockets and played pickup back in the Bronx in his spare time and occasionally at the EBC in Harlem.

One day Waliyy, who now went by the handle Main Event, called up Shane to tell him about a streetball run in New Jersey that AND 1 was going to be videotaping to put out as its followup to the Skip Mix Tape Vol. 1. Shane ended up playing well, showcasing himself as a speedy ballhandler who could put the ball through anybody's legs. But he had

the unbelievable knack of throwing pinpoint alley-oops, sometimes from as far as three-quarter court. Sometimes without even looking.

On the receiving end of many of those passes was his boy Main Event. "We just had crazy chemistry right away," said Main. "Our ability to hook up felt natural from the beginning. He always seemed to know where I was on the court and I could always tell what he was about to do. All we had to do was exchange a quick glance, then he would put the ball up there and I'd go get it."

The following summer Main and Shane became two of the six players on the initial AND 1 Mix Tape Tour and blended their quirky humor with basketball to define the early vibe of the tour.

"We were just a bunch of cats from different parks around the country and now we're playing in 10,000-seat arenas," said Main. "To stay in five-star hotels and get stopped for autographs in airports, it's just crazy. But to do it with a friend makes it all that much better."

To see more of SHANE THE DRIBBLING MACHINE, check out:

- AND 1 Mix Tape Vol. 1
- AND 1 Mix Tape Vol. 2
- AND 1 Mix Tape Vol. 3
- AND 1 Mix Tape Vol. 4
- AND 1 Mix Tape Vol. 5
- AND 1 Mix Tape Vol. 6
- AND 1 Mix Tape Vol. 7
- AND 1 Ball Access: The Mix Tape Tour
- Season 1 of ESPN's *StreetBall: The AND 1 Mix Tape Tour*
- Season 2 of ESPN's *StreetBall: The AND 1 Mix Tape Tour*

Grayson Boucher
The Professor
TOUR DEBUT: 2003

There he was at the Hyatt on Sunset Boulevard in LA at NBA All-Star weekend in February 2004. Right in the middle of the beautiful people. Loving life with wide eyes, just trying to take it all in. How the @#$% did The Professor end up here? Well, how The Professor got there is one story. How Grayson Boucher got there was entirely another.

"I couldn't even walk down the street without someone asking for my autograph," said Professor. "Everywhere we went, the game, out to eat, people were everywhere."

For a shy kid thrust into the spotlight, getting used to fame isn't quite as easy as going between his legs. After lunch at Original Pantry, a popular downtown LA diner, Grayson stepped out into the bright afternoon sunlight and two preteen girls began to point and giggle. "That's him! That's The Professor!" they whispered. The girls' mother asked Grayson if he would take a picture with her daughters. He politely complied. As the woman readied the camera it was hard to tell who was more shy, the ballplayer or the third-graders. Prime Objective eyed the scene from a few feet away and smiled.

"Gonna have to get used to that, young fella," the six-seven sage told him. "That's gonna be all day on the tour."

After a few snaps from a Nikon, the girls scurried off. Professor was left to contemplate his newfound fame.

"It's definitely fun, I can tell you that."

That's pretty much how it's been since Grayson became an overnight streetball sensation by drilling the game-winning shot at the buzzer to defeat the Mix Tape team in August 2003 in the most hallowed hoops arena in the world, Madison Square Garden. The shot helped him win the 2003 Mix Tape Tour contest in which streetball players across the country got a shot to compete on the tour from week to week, with the final contestant winning a contract to play on the official Mix Tape Tour.

"I never thought I'd play in the Garden," said Professor. "The closest I've been to that was a video game. Hitting that shot was one of the most memorable moments of my career."

That shot and that summer are history. He's

gone from Grayson to The Professor, from Salem to your living room, proving streetballers come from everywhere these days. Even places where pine trees outnumber the people.

Salem, Oregon, is a sleepy town 45 minutes southwest of Portland. Like any other kid growing up a die-hard hoops fan, Grayson had the jerseys of his favorite players. Watched Big Monday. Had his wall papered with pictures of his favorite players. Pretended he was JWill one day, AI the next.

And like a lot of other kids, Grayson wasn't exactly varsity material when he entered the ninth grade at McNary High. His freshman year, the five-eight point guard went out for the basketball team, and the coach promptly placed him on the junior varsity. He was beanpole skinny and lacked significant height. He would have been out the door save for one shining ability. No one in Salem could handle the ball like he could.

"I've always been able to dribble," he said. "But back then my game wasn't as showy. I relied on my outside shot and my floater. I didn't have the moves I have now but I've always had a certain amount of flair."

But something happened during his freshman year that would change his life. A friend showed him a copy of Mix Tape Vol. 2. He watched it until the tape would no longer play, over and over until the moves were ingrained on his mind.

"I couldn't believe what I was watching," he said. "At first I didn't know who the players were. But then I was like 'Skip to My Lou is the man.'"

Around that time Grayson started playing ball at Marion Park—nothing special, but it's where Salem's best street run took place. Soon he had one of the most complete street arsenals in the Portland area: crossovers, hands up, ball tricks. "The tapes totally changed the way I looked at basketball," said Grayson. "My whole game opened up because all of a sudden I had this creativity. The tapes were so inspirational I felt like a new door had opened."

Soon he got his hands on Mix Tape Vol. 1 and devoted more time to sharpening his moves. Though his skills improved, he still wasn't getting any shine with McNary no matter how much he held his street game back. Coach kept him on JV until his junior year. Not good for a five-eight point guard looking for a college ride.

Grayson hired a local dribbling coach named Rodney Howard and transferred to the smaller, more exclusive Salem Academy his senior year for more exposure. The move paid off as he averaged 20 points and 7 assists (including a 38-point outburst in a state playoff game) and led his team to a second-place finish in the Tri River Conference. He was named third-team all-state and second-team all-region. Gray wrapped up his high-school career by playing in the Oregon 2A Boys All-Star game. Despite the fact that he was named second-team all-state, no college came knocking. "I guess they thought I wasn't that important," said Grayson.

Although he got no national love, a local paper hinted at what was to come. "Boucher teases defenders with his blinding ball-handling skills and attempts passes that frequently befuddle even his own teammates," wrote the *Statesman Journal* (Salem, Oregon) of Gray in 2002.

In the fall Grayson walked on to Chemeketa Junior College in Oregon. While he didn't get the run he wanted, his coach was pleased with his effort.

"Grayson did a good job," said Chemekeda assistant coach David Abderhalden. "What he lacks in size (135 pounds) he makes up for with intelligence."

After his freshman year, Gray had set up a job for himself at a local grocery store. He thought he'd stack some minor paper in between getting his game sharp for next season.

"I was planning to work in a grocery store in the summer of 2003 so this is much cooler," Boucher says. "To tell you the truth I wasn't looking forward to working there but I would have done it. I hated working the register because people are always complaining about the job you're doing. Even though I didn't like it, I think it really taught me something. Every time I go into a grocery store and somebody messes up I don't give them a hard time because I know exactly where they are coming from."

But all Gray wanted to do was play ball. He wasn't into scanning coupons and couldn't care less whether the eggs went on top of the watermelon or the other way around. In between pickup games and marathon Mix Tape viewings he checked AND 1's website for tour info. When he learned that the tour would be at Memorial Coliseum in Portland on June 16, 2003, he marked the calendar and polished his crossover.

On the day of the tour, he grabbed his 15-year-old brother, Landon, jumped in the car, and headed for action.

"He didn't even tell us where he was going," said his mother, Molly. "But when he got home he was so excited."

Excited is how you could describe the reaction of those in attendance when the unassuming 19-year-old came to life on the parking-lot asphalt. On one trip he caught a rebound in midair and faked a forward pass in the same motion. Upon returning to earth he faked a behind-the-back pass to the right then funneled one off in the opposite direction (see *StreetBall*, Season 2, Episode 3).

"That was pretty much all we needed to see," said Mix Tape Tour team member Prime Objective, who helped select Grayson that day for the indoor run. "There was something about him. He was doing stuff a lot of us hadn't seen and we've been at this a long time."

Grayson quickly established himself as one of the hottest players on the tour, and by the game at the Garden, it was evident that he was the man to beat. A clear sign he was on his way was that he had impressed tour MC Duke Tango enough to have the legendary game caller bestow a nickname upon him. Tango decided on The Professor.

"Because he takes people to school like no other," says Tango.

Duke has named nearly every streetball player of note in New York City. That summer he named his first from Salem, Oregon.

"I wasn't sure I liked it when I first heard Duke say it," Grayson recalled. "But everyone else started saying it and it seemed to catch on pretty quickly."

"We think it's so cute," said Mom. "It fits him perfectly."

By the middle of the tour, ESPN began running the episodes of *StreetBall*, which chronicled the tour and its *American Idol/Survivor*–like streetball contest. "The first time I saw myself on TV it was kind of weird," said Grayson, "but I got used to it pretty quickly. When I'd be at home all I did was check the TV guide for when *StreetBall* would come on. I'd watch the show and try to imagine millions of people across the country watching it at the same exact moment. The best episode was the one in New Orleans when my dad came down. He got just as big a kick out of it as I did."

On the tour, Professor has endeared himself to fans and teammates alike with his boy-next-door charm and genuine humility. "That's just the way I was raised," Grayson said. "That's how my parents raised me and my brother."

The Toronto stop on the tour held special significance for the kid from Salem. He would finally come face to face with the man whom he had watched on those Mix Tapes a thousand times before. The tapes had been one thing, but when he walked onto the court with Skip to My Lou, it was a whole different game. "I couldn't believe I was looking at him, about to play with him," said Professor. "I'd watch the Mix Tapes and wish I could play with Skip. I knew he was going to get me, but if you play against Skip, you're going to end up on the highlight tape."

The kid from Salem held his own, delighting the crowd with his patented hesitation, herky-jerky crossover. At the end of the game the legend and the neophyte met at center court.

"It was great playing against you," Skip said.

"I'm so honored to meet you, thanks for everything," replied Grayson, taken aback by the moment.

With that the Queens native walked off. Grayson stood for a few moments wearing a look of disbelief. He had just played against the guy who up until now had just been a grainy image on his television screen, a myth whose exploits traveled only by word of mouth. From 155th to his living room.

Now not only did he know Skip was real, Skip knew about *him* too.

So now you know how he got there. And you can't take your eyes off him because you want to see where he's going.

"You know what's crazy?" Grayson asks. "Some little kid is going watch the new Mix Tapes and copy my moves and want to meet me, too."

And when you see him, tell him thanks.

To see more of THE PROFESSOR, check out:

- AND 1 Mix Tape Vol. 6 (very limited appearance)
- AND 1 Mix Tape Vol. 7
- Season 2 of ESPN's *Streetball: The AND 1 Mix Tape Tour*

Robin Kennedy
Sik Wit It
TOUR DEBUT: 2001

Ask Robin Kennedy and he'll tell you the west side is the best side. Coming from Pasadena, the baller better known as Sik Wit It is the lone AND 1 original who wasn't raised on the blacktop of the East. "No disrespect to anybody in the East," said Sik, "but we've been holding it down out here for years." The 30-year-old Kennedy began honing his skills at the Pasadena Boys & Girls club where he could be found most days driving hard on defenders twice his size and bombing from so far out you had to catch a cab to go out and check him.

When his game had further developed, Kennedy took his skills to one of the hottest spots in LA—the courts at Venice Beach. Every Saturday and Sunday he and his boy Reggie Cotton would trek 45 minutes south of Pasadena to LA. But the regulars there didn't quite respond to his scrappy style of play. "I just needed the chance to hold my own against the big boys," said Kennedy, who was 14 when he first stepped on the court at Venice. "I was never nervous to play with older players. A lot of kids were, but I wasn't."

Sik constantly worked on his game and felt he could have had a shot at starting when he entered Pasadena High as a freshman. But right away things went wrong. To say he and the coach didn't get along is putting it nicely. "He claimed I had an attitude problem," remembered Sik. "He tried to act more like my father than a coach and I wasn't having that."

Things came to a head when Sik's entire family came to see

him play and he only got about two minutes of burn. The next day in practice Sik confronted his coach about it and was promptly tossed out of practice. And that was it for Pasadena High. The following year he transferred to Lynwood Adventist Academy, a private, mostly black school, where he flourished in a fast-paced offense. He averaged 26 points a game in his sophomore year at Lynwood and quickly emerged as one of the top prospects in Southern California.

Like every budding high-school prospect, Robin was a regular on the summer camp scene. Nike, Pump Brothers, and Michael Cooper's camp were some of the places where you could find him in the summer season. One summer he met a young point guard five years his junior in whom Sik saw a lot of potential. He decided to ask the kid for his autograph. The kid signed a towel "Baron Davis future McDonald's All American." Five years later Davis became the All-American he predicted he would be, and today Sik still has the towel.

After leading Lynwood to the California State finals in his senior year, he was recruited by George Tarkanian, son of Jerry and head coach of Chaffey College, one of the top JUCOs in California. Tark set him up with an apartment and got him into school. As a package deal, Tark agreed to take Sik's boy Reggie Cotton to give the school a lethal one-two punch.

Chaffey played in one of the better JUCO leagues in the country, satisfying Kennedy's thirst for top competition. In November 1994, Chaffey faced Saddleback Community College, matching Robin up with future NBA guard Anthony Carter. Saddleback won 78–68 behind Carter's 31 points. Kennedy pumped in 24 points of his own. "Looking back I'd have to say it was a great matchup," said Kennedy. "I never shied away from challenging the top guys." The team finished 32–6 in his freshman year.

The highlight of his sophomore season, in which Chaffey went 28–9, was their matchup with Ventura junior college and its star point guard Rafer Alston. "I had never heard of him and it wasn't until a few years later when I found out what he was all about," said Sik. "But looking back it all made sense because that boy could play."

Ventura ended Kennedy's hopes for a JUCO state championship and his days at Chaffey.

In a junior college all-star game (sponsored by AND 1) held at the Pyramid in Long Beach, Robin showed scouts from Fresno State and UNLV, among others, how he could mix flash with organized ball by handing out 15 assists, including several alley-oops from halfcourt. On the last play of the game, the five-eleven guard drove the lane and jumped into the arms of the six-six Cotton, who hoisted him in the air for the two-handed throw-down.

"That was us just having fun and me showing my personality and skills," Sik said. In the crowd were members of the University of Nevada–Reno's coaching staff, who extended Kennedy a scholarship offer. Jerry Tarkanian wanted him to walk on at Fresno State but that meant that he had to pay his own way to school. He decided to go with a sure thing.

While Cotton went on to Cal-Bakersfield, Sik accepted a scholarship to play D1 ball at Nevada. In the beginning of his junior year, the 1996–97 season, disaster struck. During a preseason practice, a teammate fell on his leg, resulting in a gruesome tear in the ACL in his left knee. His season was over before it even started.

"It was really depressing because I really wanted to prove myself to everyone that I could play on this level," he said.

The following year Kennedy finally got a chance to show his ability as the team's starting point guard and averaged 14.6 points and a league-leading 6.7 assists. In the WAC conference finals, Nevada faced Pacific and that year's number-one NBA pick, Michael Olowokandi. "He just killed us," remembered Sik. "We had no answer for him inside."

After graduating from Nevada, he went back to Pasadena and the Boys & Girls club, looking for some run and looking for work. Jobs were hard to come by. San Diego Wild Fire head coach LaSalle Thompson asked Sik if he had any interest in playing in the new ABA, which was up and running in the spring of 2000.

Complete with red, white, and blue ball, the ABA represented a new beginning for Kennedy.

Robin looked at it as the perfect opportunity to continue to hone his game in hopes of getting that one shot at the league. He signed on with a team that included a former LSU center, seven-foot, 340-pound Stanley Roberts.

"To me that whole situation was politically incorrect," Sik said. "There were guys that they wanted to get back into the league and they played them before me."

One of those guys was former Boston Celtic Marlon Garnett. "You can't tell me he was better than me," said Sik. "I outplayed him on a nightly basis."

Sik says the coach went from being cool to a chump. Thompson even drove Sik to his first game but rarely played him. "I just got tired of sitting when I was proving myself in practice." He left San Diego in the middle of the season and headed back for Pasadena.

In July 2000, Sik went to LA's Bel Air Park, where AND 1 was holding tryouts for a spot to compete against the fledgling Mix Tape team the next day at Southwest College. Sik impressed the scouts and was asked to compete.

He was pumped about the opportunity but almost didn't make it. "I couldn't get a ride to the game," Sik recalled.

But he eventually made it and was surprised to see his teammates were nervous about playing against AND 1's collection of legends.

"But I wasn't nervous one bit," he said. "It's just basketball."

Sik was matched for most of the game against a streetball star from Atlanta named Hot Sauce who was also making his AND 1 debut. Immediately after the game, Sik signed a contract to tour the country on the Mix Tape bus.

Since then his Rob K crossover and comic relief have been a welcome addition to the Mix Tape Tour. Another unexpected advantage of having Sik on board has been his vocal cords.

"We're just so used to him singing every day," said Hot Sauce, "it wouldn't seem right without hearing his voice."

In March 2004, Sik put his talent to good use when he sang the gospel song "To God Be the Glory" at the funeral of Antoine "Flash" Howard, former Mix Tape team member and one of his closest friends.

"That was one of the most important moments in my life," said Sik.

At 30, Sik is one of the elder statesmen on the streetball scene, but is nowhere near ready to give up the game he loves.

"Basketball is what I do," said Sik, "and you can bet I'll be doing this for a long time to come."

To see more of SIK WIT IT, check out:

- AND 1 Mix Tape Vol. 5
- AND 1 Mix Tape Vol. 6
- AND 1 Mix Tape Vol. 7
- AND 1 Ball Access: The Mix Tape Tour
- Season 1 of ESPN's *StreetBall: The AND 1 Mix Tape Tour*
- Season 2 of ESPN's *StreetBall: The AND 1 Mix Tape Tour*

Waliyy Dixon
Main Event
TOUR DEBUT: 2000

And in this corner...

The kid should have been a boxer. That's what his father, Wallace Dixon, used to think. He was larger than the other kids and at 10 had the reach of kids five years his senior. Today Waliyy is six-four, 220 pounds with broad shoulders. Dad may have been on to something. But when Waliyy picked up a basketball at nine years of age, that put an end to that. This Jersey-bred baller was born in Elizabeth and raised in Linden, where he honed his streetball game at 4th Ward.

In July 1989, Waliyy's 17-and-under AAU squad competed in a tournament in Kingsport, Tennessee. He made the all-tournament team with averages of 22.5 points and 13 rebounds in seven games. The numbers were nice but fans could leave a game they had just seen Waliyy play in and have no idea how many points he scored. All they could talk about were his half a dozen Superman dunks.

His reputation for getting plenty of face time with the rim was becoming widespread throughout Jersey, and by the time he entered his senior year he was ranked as one of the top 15 high school players in America by the recruiting mag *Hoop Scoop*. He was also named Street and Smith honorable mention. Waliyy had received a lot of attention from Big East and Atlantic 10 schools but he was pursued the hardest by Rutgers.

Dixon didn't waste any time deciding where he wanted to go to school.

"I knew I wanted to stay close to home," said Dixon. "That was important to me because I wanted to stay near my grandmother."

"The guy reminds me of David Thompson, he flies," said Rutgers head coach Bob Wenzel, who coached against the former North Carolina State All-American while at Duke, to the *Bergen Record* in 1991. "He'll take off from the foul line, glide through the air with the ball in his left hand, and just dunk over everybody. He's a terribly exciting player. He can be a top, top, top college player, and maybe beyond."

On October 14, 1991, Waliyy signed a letter of intent to play at Rutgers. It was a major coup for the school. By the end of the season scouts generally regarded him as the second-best player in the state behind Kentucky-bound Roderick Rhodes of St. Anthony's. To cap his season he was named second-team all-state. But that's where the good news ended. Waliyy had taken care of business on the court but the classroom was another issue. He had yet to score the 700 on his SAT that incoming college freshman needed to be eligible to play.

By July before his freshman year he had yet to make the score and faced an all-too-typical tough decision: sit out and pay your own way or go the JUCO and be eligible immediately. Dixon agonized over the decision all summer. He considered several junior colleges and even told local reporters that his going to Rutgers wasn't going to work out.

"Waliyy was in a position where he needed to do what was best for him, but he knows there's a place for him here," said Wenzel. "We loved him as a player, but it was his decision."

The coach's commitment to the Linden ballplayer was what swayed him to keep his commitment to Rutgers. But getting through that first year wouldn't be easy. Prop 48 players aren't permitted to play or practice.

Another blow was the departure of Jeff Van Gundy and Eddie Jordan, leaving Waliyy without the coaches who recruited him and the men he looked up to.

During Rutgers Midnight Madness on October 15, 1992, Waliyy was on the sidelines. He was relegated to a student slam-dunk contest, which he won. The bright spot was that it gave the fans something to look forward to.

Dixon returned for his sophomore campaign to average 9.6 points and four rebounds on 34 percent from the field despite dealing with nagging injuries for most of the season.

But in summer 1994, after Waliyy's sophomore season, he was once again removed from the team for academic reasons. His career at Rutgers was done. He headed for Benedict College in South Carolina, where he had family to keep his mind right. But Benedict turned out to be just another stop on the winding basketball turnpike that was his career.

After college he became a regular at Rucker Park. At first he went by the moniker Main Attraction. Then he met Duke Tango.

"He was in the layup line one evening at the Rucker," said Tango, "when he threw down a dunk so vicious, with so much authority I just stopped in my tracks. Right there I said he's no longer the main attraction, he's the Main Event."

Other stops on his odyssey through basketball's underbelly included the Harlem Wizards *and* Harlem Rockets, where he

teamed with his pal Shane The Dribbling Machine to battle pow-erhouses like the Pulaski Muggles. The Sacramento Kings they weren't.

"That's just what I had to do at the time," said Main. "I had to eat and basketball was how I knew I could put food on the table. Some of those situations weren't the best but I learned to deal with them."

When the original Mix Tape session took place at Waliyy's home court in Linden, he knew this was his time to shine. "I just came out and balled like I normally did," he said. "Shane's passes were on point and it just seemed like everybody brought their A material."

On the Mix Tape Tour Waliyy's veteran leadership is just as valued as his thunderous throwdowns. The tour in return has given him a new perspective on life. "If the league ain't meant for me then that's life," said Waliyy. "I can deal with that. With the tour I'm still getting paid to play ball. This is my life; all I ever wanted was a chance."

Basketball is the path he chose. And there's no getting off. Just call his cell. His voice mail greets callers with, "You've reached Main Event...AND 1...baller for life."

Please leave a message.

To see more MAIN EVENT, check out:

- AND 1 Mix Tape Vol. 1
- AND 1 Mix Tape Vol. 2
- AND 1 Mix Tape Vol. 3
- AND 1 Mix Tape Vol. 4
- AND 1 Mix Tape Vol. 5
- AND 1 Mix Tape Vol. 6
- AND 1 Mix Tape Vol. 7
- AND 1 Ball Access: The Mix Tape Tour
- Season 1 of ESPN's *StreetBall: The AND 1 Mix Tape Tour*
- Season 2 of ESPN's *StreetBall: The AND 1 Mix Tape Tour*

Robert Martin "50"

TOUR DEBUT: 2001

Born in Atlanta on January 6, 1973, and raised in College Park, Georgia, Robert "50" Martin was almost always about basketball. As a kid he played some little-league football, but didn't stick with it. "I didn't get the ball that much, and we wasn't winning any games, so I quit," said Martin.

So basketball became his thing. Coming from humble beginnings, Martin was kept in line by a mom who did the job of two parents. And being the youngest of six children—three brothers and two sisters—meant plenty of other family members had their eye on him.

"My mom and dad got divorced, and my mom raised six kids, and I was the youngest. I lived in the projects, you know what I mean? It was rough growing up, bad neighborhood, but my mom just kept my head on right. I listened to her and just managed to stay out of trouble, and tried to stick to my dream of playing basketball. Basketball kept me out of trouble, you know. I had a lot of friends get in trouble and things like that. Got caught up in bad situations. So I just learned to stay away from that. I just used to come home from school and go to the gym, and come back home.

"I moved when I was three to College Park, Georgia. It's like a suburb, outside of Atlanta. And that's where I grew up at. The main gym there was Brady Gym. That's where I learned to play," said Martin.

In high school, Martin began his basketball career as a point guard at College Park High. "Our high school started in eighth grade and I started at point guard," Martin said.

Martin had only grown to six-one by the 10th grade when he first started throwing down on people's heads. It was around that time when his coach started using him at almost every position. Regardless of size, kids couldn't check him. He was too quick, too strong, too fast.

"In 10th grade I averaged 15 points. In 11th grade about 13. By my senior year I averaged 20 points per game," said Martin.

College was a step-by-step procedure for Martin. "A lot of schools wanted me. St. Bonaventure, Western Kentucky. But I ended up going to junior college for two years. Middle Georgia College. I was waiting on the other schools to give me an answer of what they were going to do, if they were going to sign me or not, but it got to the point that I couldn't wait anymore."

The two years (1991–93) at junior college weren't too exciting for Martin. The school is about two hours south of Atlanta and in the middle of nowhere. But he made the most of it. "It had a dead environment, you know what I mean?" Martin said. "But I enjoyed it, I sucked it up."

After his two years at Middle Georgia were up, Martin moved on to High Point University in North Carolina. Although the school is now in the Big South Conference, it was Division 2 basketball in Martin's days.

The highlight of his High Point tenure was snagging Division 2 player of the week in January 1995 with a pair of near triple double performances.

By this time, the basketball world had taken notice of Martin's skills. In 1995, he was drafted by the Atlanta Trojans of the USBL. Plenty of older players on the team meant that his minutes would be limited. The USBL season is short and only goes through the summer, so he quickly needed another paying hoop gig.

This need took him across the ocean.

A professional basketball opportunity in Europe was calling, and he wasn't about to miss out. In December 1995, he went to Luxembourg to play for Palma-Ahn. What Martin delivered was nothing short of domination.

In 1995–96, he put up about 33 points per game, won Luxembourg's Slam Dunk Championship, and also played in the All-Star game. The next season he copped averages of 35 points and 12 rebounds per game. In 1998, he topped 40 points per game, one of the best seasons in club history. Although his team always did well, finishing high up in the standings, Palma-Ahn didn't win a championship during Martin's run.

He left Palma-Ahn in 1998, returned to the United States, and signed on with Team Georgia, a traveling exhibition team.

"We played exhibitions against college teams, for the preseason. I played for a year until I heard about a new league coming out called the IBL. I went to the predraft camp and I was in the top 20 out of 460 players," recalled Martin.

He was assigned to the New Mexico Slam camp. "I did pretty well, but they didn't pick me up," he said. "I think politics got involved with it. I was very unhappy because I knew I should have made the squad. But I was there without a team."

In the winter of 1999, he played in the IBA for the Rochester Skeeters in Rochester, Minnesota. He played for two months and averaged 12 points, seven rebounds. But he didn't mesh with the coach.

"Man, we couldn't get along," recalled Robert with disdain. "So in January 2000, my coach [in Luxembourg] from Palma-Ahn went to another team and he wanted me to come play for him. I was in a tough situation playing in the IBA, but I told the coach from Europe that I'd come back to play for him if he got me a ticket out of Minnesota." He was on a plane the next day.

The IBA was a lost cause, but he did get one thing out of Rochester. Some of his friends used to loudly point out to everyone within earshot that Martin could jump 40 inches. To Martin it was more like 50. Thanks to heavy promotion from street legend Ed "Booger" Smith, an IBA teammate of Martin's, the matter was settled. It was 50.

After another European gig, he headed back to Georgia. "That's when AND 1 started doing their tour. And later on, during the summer, one of my friends was telling me that AND 1 was coming up to the gym and they was looking for some players."

"I was telling my friend, 'Man, I've been up in this gym all day, I'm thinking about going home.'" So he ended up staying, and they had the little open run at Atlanta's Run-n-Shoot, where 50 impressed by throwing down three consecutive alley-oop slams. They invited him to play in the AND 1 game at Morris Brown college.

In 2001, he played on the tour for four games and began winning over fans with his jackhammer throwdowns and toothy grin. In February 2002, AND 1 offered him a contract and the rest in streetball history.

"My role is to play defense, block shots, get rebounds, get out on the break, do exciting dunks, throw it off the shot clock, whatever," 50 said. "I get the crowd into the game.

"I'm the type of player, I don't have attitude, I get along with everybody, and I think I'm known for scoring a lot of points, but I'll never get comfortable with my game. Each year I just try to keep improving, and add something to my game."

His vertical is one area he won't have to worry about.

To see more of "50," check out:

- AND 1 Mix Tape Vol. 5
- AND 1 Mix Tape Vol. 6
- AND 1 Mix Tape Vol. 7
- AND 1 Ball Access: The Mix Tape Tour
- Season 1 of ESPN's *StreetBall: The AND 1 Mix Tape Tour*
- Season 2 of ESPN's *StreetBall: The AND 1 Mix Tape Tour*

John Harvey
High Octane
TOUR DEBUT: 2001

The rim is your enemy. Smash it with all your might. Layups should be illegal. Weak dunks shoudn't even count. Dunk. Hard. Hit the iron so hard, the Earth's rotation speeds up. Or slows down. When the rock needs to be thrown down with authority, there's a Bronx-born bomber who thinks he's the man for the job.

Being a New Yorker means having to represent. Having to go up strong every time, because the world knows New York City, and much is expected of basketball players who emerge from the concrete boroughs. Nobody knows this more than John Harvey, AND 1's six-eight rim inspector who goes by the street name High Octane. Represent NYC, always. New Yorkers are known for being cocky. They have to perform, no matter where they are. Octane has always felt this pressure, but it's not a problem—he embraces it and has always used it as motivation. No matter where he's been, any time he had a bad game, somehow he'd wind up hearing about it from guys back home in the Bronx. He could be messing around at some court in the middle of nowhere and return to NYC a few days later, and somehow cats around the hood knew he failed to rep the hood.

Making a name for himself in basketball is what always drove Octane. He heard stories of Connie Hawkins and wanted to be him. Wanted to soar like him. Finish like him above clouds. Stars like Main Event, Skip to My Lou, Speedy Claxton, and other guys who earned their legacies at the playground and, in some cases, well beyond motivated Octane to strive to be as great as he could be. Lloyd "Sweet Pea" Daniels, too. Everybody, everywhere. If a player had New York roots, that just made him more special in Octane's eyes. And he's proud to know his name is in that highly respected group of famous streetballers who cut their teeth in NYC.

Born in the boogie-down Bronx on January 19, 1978, and raised there all his life, Octane came from a clan of family and friends that lived and breathed basketball. Everyone he knew and hung out with balled, constantly. By age three, Harvey was working on developing a handle bouncing a ball a third his size.

Basketball wasn't his only game as a kid. He briefly played baseball, but the sport wasn't for him. The entire flow of the game just wasn't right. At age seven he played shortstop in little league but he left being a minibomber to the other kids when he kept getting drilled in the chin.

From that point on, it was all about basketball.

Growng up with his mother and brother, and not much of a father, in Parkchester on the 11th floor of an average Bronx building, there weren't a lot of famous rappers or ballers hanging around like you see in videos. His block, and surrounding blocks, lacked the star power of Alimoe's Harlem world. Just regular people working hard, and plenty of others hardly working.

When Oc was 16 and playing in the Frederick Douglass tournament in the Bronx for coach Vic Hall, his point guard tossed an errant alley-oop pass over his head and out of bounds. Or so everyone thought. To Octane, it was a normal pass.

As the ball was heading out of bounds, Octane soared, reached back behind his head with one hand, and somehow managed to maintain control and slam the ball through the rim. Think Grant Hill against Kansas in the 1991 Final Four.

"The coaches I was playing against, they wanted to check that I was the right age," said Octane. "They'd never seen a kid rise like that."

Octane entered Christopher Columbus High in the Bronx and

went out for the squad. As a freshman he played junior varsity and put up around 10 points per game. It was a modest average, but during the season he caught the eye of varsity coach Howard Kaplan. Coach Kaplan saw talent and potential. He liked the way he could establish position on the block and execute a pick and roll.

But the two had a distinct difference of opinion when it came to the playing time Octane would receive as a sophomore on the varsity squad. Coach saw a kid to bring off the bench, at least for the season: Let him put on some weight and sharpen his J in the off-season. But the player wanted to start. For him, having him coming off the bench was disrespecting his game. But in high-school, basketball coaches rule. Rather than deal with it, Octane stuck with the junior varsity team as a sophomore. He regulated the comp, putting 20 in the books each night.

In order to get the type of run he wanted, he had to work on his game. Subway and bus tokens were his ticket to the best basket-ball New York City had to offer. Octane made his mark at Rucker Park, Dyckman, and wherever he could find serious competition. In his junior season, and first on varsity, he put up 13 a game and Coach Kaplan couldn't keep him out of the game. As a senior, it got serious: 18 points, 11 rebounds, 5 smack backs, and the attention of lower Division 1 schools.

Sienna wanted him. So did Sacred Heart, Iona, and others. He chose Long Island University, C.W. Post campus, run by coach Tom Galleazzi.

But first he spent a season at Sullivan Community College in upstate New York. He immediately became Sullivan's star, putting up 20 and 10 an outing. The team made it to the National JUCO Final Four. Then it was off to C.W. Post for the remainder of Octane's college eligibility.

In 2001, a few months after his senior year ended, the tour had come to Riverside Park on the Upper West Side. With the summer almost over, there was no way Octane would miss the game. He was asked to play, represented properly, and turned heads. Shane The Dribbling Machine urged Octane to hit the tour's remaining cities to close the summer. Octane traveled to Chicago and Los Angeles, playing well in both games. AND 1 knew they had a player worth keeping, and contract negotiations began almost immediately. By the end of 2001, High Octane was officially with AND 1.

Octane sees the squad as a family, but family time is suspended temporarily when you hit the court.

"When we're playing against each other, it's something out of a comic book," Octane said. "It's like Superman meets Batman, and you're fighting for that pride, you know what I'm sayin'? We're always friends, we're like brothers, we fight and argue too but it's all love. After the game you bury the hatchet. But believe me, we're on the court, we're at war. We're definitely at war."

"If you're not out there trying to prove that you're the best that anyone can play against, you don't belong out there. Plus, people are going to test you anyway, to see where your heart is at. They're definitely going to test you all of the time when you step on that court."

Octane understands the responsibility that comes with being a streetball legend. There's a bull's-eye on him at all times. A target on his back. And he wouldn't have it any other way.

"I'm an attack-the-rim kind of guy. Give me an inch and I'm taking a mile. I'm taking the whole enchilada. I'm attacking the rim. I'm trying to tear the rim down. Dunking hard. I go hard. It's not going to be a soft dunk. It's going to be a hard, powerful dunk. That's really how I got my name. They call me High Octane because I jump high and when I dunk it's like an explosion."

In 2003, when the tour brought him to a faraway land called Australia, a place on the other side of the planet where water swirls in the wrong direction and Russell Crowe is king, fans knew him. They rushed to him. He was famous. He couldn't have been farther from the Bronx. Still, fans down under knew exactly who he was. And Aussies got no love for weak dunks.

To see more of HIGH OCTANE, check out:

- AND 1 Mix Tape Vol. 5
- AND 1 Mix Tape Vol. 6
- AND 1 Mix Tape Vol. 7
- AND 1 Ball Access: The Mix Tape Tour
- Season 1 of ESPN's *StreetBall: The AND 1 Mix Tape Tour*
- Season 2 of ESPN's *StreetBall: The AND 1 Mix Tape Tour*

John Humphrey
Helicopter
TOUR DEBUT: 2003

Have you ever seen someone jump so high that when they come down their shoes are out of style? Then you've never seen the Helicopter. If he counted the heads he's flushed on he'd have to hire a census taker. "Dunking is just something that's always been a part of my game," said Helicopter. "It's a part of the game that everybody wants to see."

John "Helicopter" Humphrey was born on September 8, 1980, in Morehead City, North Carolina. Playing sports mostly right around Grandma's house, Helicopter tried every sport and physical activity imaginable.

He first dunked in a sixth-grade PE class, to the amazement of his teachers and classmates. Around that time he occasionally stayed with his uncle, who had an 11-foot goal in his driveway. "The thing about it was that you had to run uphill to dunk," said Humphries. By the time he reached high school he could dunk the 11-foot rim easily.

In ninth grade, playing his first organized basketball, he began his hoop life as a shooting guard who occasionally filled in at small forward. Helicopter honed his ball handling and jump-shot on West Carteret High's junior varsity. From his sophomore year on he began to develop real basketball skills and the confidence he needed to take things to higher levels.

"That's when I started to dunk on a regular basis," he said. "I seemed like I just kept going higher and higher."

Small-town basketball proved too easy for Helicopter. The competition—or lack there-of—was not challenging. To be the best, you have to battle the best. So rather than spend his senior year destroying inferior competition, he transferred to Oak Hill Academy in Mouth of Wilson, Virginia, to play for coach Steve Smith.

It was the right move. And while Oak Hill's games were good experience, practice was even better. It was there that Helicopter was matched up against the best competition, his own teammates. Actual Oak Hill games were often blowouts, but the real action was in practice scrimmages.

Scrimmages with the likes of future Maryland and Washington Wizards point guard Steve Blake and former Tennessee star Ron Slay were some of the best runs of his life. But he got the most work going against Cliff Hawkins, who went on to play four years at Kentucky.

Sometimes Oak Hill ran a two-minute drill with one team down five to see if they could come back. The drill was intended to get the players to go against each other as hard as they could.

In December of his senior year Oak Hill played a tournament in Las Vegas, where Helicopter stole the show from his more heralded teammates. He came off the bench in a 101–54 thumping of Horizon and put together a string of five highlight-reel dunks in seven minutes.

"I've coached 20 years and he is the greatest dunker I've ever seen," said Oak Hill coach Steve Smith.

The prep powerhouse finished the 1998–99 season with a perfect 31–0 record and captured

the elusive mythical national championship. Helicopter averaged 11.1 points and 4.1 rebounds, and got the most out of his senior season.

Georgetown wanted him. So did most other schools in the Big East. And he was happy to accommodate them. But with a new little baby girl back in North Carolina, he wanted a school close to home. He wound up attending Louisburg Junior College, a private, Methodist-affiliated college in Louisburg, North Carolina. Under the leadership of coach Enid Drake, Helicopter continued to blossom. Drake, who once coached Blue Edwards and two-time

All-American Russell Davis, often kept Helicopter after practice to work on his fundamentals.

It paid off. Junior college competition was no match for Helicopter, as he averaged 22 points per game. Things got even more serious in his sophomore year: 24.6 points and 5.3 rebounds per game. He was named third-team JUCO All-American and was voted team MVP both years at the school.

After two seasons at Louisburg, Helicopter looked to attend the University of Oklahoma. But Randy Wiel, head coach of Middle Tennessee State University, located in Murfreesboro, talked with him into joining MT. The team ran an offense similar to the one Helicopter was familiar with from his high-school days, so he fit right in. Helicopter's first year as a Blue Raider was an adjustment period. In 17.7 minutes per game he averaged 7.3 points and 2.1 rebounds.

In his senior season, Coach Wiel was out the door, replaced by Kermit Davis. Helicopter started, putting up 9.2 points and 4.8 rebounds in 26 minutes per game as the team went 16–14.

A few months after he was out of school, the 2003 AND 1 Mix Tape Tour was making its way around the country. When the tour stopped in Raleigh, Helicopter was ready to fly. "I was nervous but I was used to playing in front of crowds and strong competition," he said.

In that Raleigh open run, Helicopter made sure to do the little things as well as bring the big flushes and was invited to play in the real game. The man made it happen and got to stick with the tour's "visitors" team till the end.

Helicopter doesn't change his game for anybody, not even AND 1. "If you watch the Mix Tapes, I play the fundamentals," he said. "I do the same things I do in a real game: shoot the shot, pass the ball, go to the hoop. I leave tricks and stuff for Hot Sauce and them."

First on Helicopter's basketball agenda is winning. Second is keeping the crowd involved. Making them happy. Giving both

fans and teammates what they want. He does what it takes,
whether it's flushing on somebody, making it rain from outside,
or scraping his dome piece on the backboard to block a shot.

"I really don't have a signature move, to be honest with you. I
just do whatever it takes to get everybody into it. If it takes dunking on somebody, then okay, that's what happens. Shooting a
deep three, I can do that too."

A solid bond formed between Helicopter and the other traveling AND 1 "visiting team" ballers, Professor and Spyda, last summer. While everyone was pushing the three to compete against
one another they instead became close.

Helicopter's also a fan of his more accomplished counterparts.
"I love the way AO plays," Helicopter said. "He could be in the
NBA, I think. The way he changes directions is unheard of, just
crazy. Escalade can really play as well. He's agile, he can move,
he'd be scary if he'd lose 100 pounds. Sik Wit It's got a lot of han-
dles and he always changes his game and adds more stuff to it."

In the winter of 2004 he kept his game tight by running with the Las Vegas Rattlers of the ABA, a team that also featured Master P and was coached by Joe "Jellybean" Bryant, Kobe's pop. He laid 26 a game on Sin City and has an open invitation to return when he's not on the tour.

He and P became close friends and Helicopter has made cameo appearances in two of his videos. Since leaving Las Vegas the two have been in weekly contact and P regularly leaves tickets for Helicopter whenever he's in town for a concert.

Helicopter jelled with Coach Bryant, who could be described as player friendly. "He still has the mentality of a player and really lets guys play through their mistakes," Helicopter said.

Push him and the six-one, 205-pound Helicopter will serve up a scouting report on himself: "I can go to the basket hard and I can shoot the ball so you have to deny me every time," Helicopter said. "I've been working my whole life, everybody wants to grow up shooting the three but I can put it on the ground with either hand. Pretty simple."

OK, so that's all he's giving up.

Off the court he likes to keep things simple, too. "I stay home, relax, wash my car. I'm from the country, so the city life ain't really for me," he said. "I'm a mellow type guy."

Still, watch ya head.

To see more of HELICOPTER, check out:

- AND 1 Mix Tape Vol. 7
- Season 2 of ESPN's *StreetBall: The AND 1 Mix Tape Tour*

Tony Jones
Go Get It

TOUR DEBUT: 2003

Life in Chicago's Hyde Park area was as rough-and-tumble as life can be. Gangs ran the streets. But Tony Jones did his best to avoid confrontation. He balled at a court known as the Lakefront, located on Lake Shore Drive a few minutes from home. The famous court, which Scottie Pippen and others have blessed, was mostly devoid of gangs. When not playing there, Jones could be found at the local YMCA.

His dad, a famous streetballer in Chicago nicknamed PT—which usually stood for Prime Time, sometimes Prince Tony—had his son playing basketball by age seven. PT played Division 3 ball at Prairie State and even get some shine in an NBA summer league run, and his skills rubbed off on his boy.

Jones lost many friends to the violent streets. Thanks to basketball and his father's street cred, he was able to avoid trouble from gangs. "They all knew who I was, because my dad is well known in the streets of Chicago," said Jones. "I wasn't bothered too much but I felt some pressure to join a gang because it's a neighborhood thing. If you live in that neighborhood, then it's either you gotta ride with those who you know, or you're just going to be an outsider and they're going to look at you as an outsider. I didn't have the type of problem where I would get beat up every day to get in a game or anything like that."

In Chi-Town, as in many cities, basketball can sometimes make you exempt from the pressures of street life.

"You have a ghetto pass if you're playing basketball, pretty much. If you're playing ball, everybody knows you, so for the most part that's your pass of getting away with a lot of things in the neighborhood."

As a high-school freshman at Chicago Vocational School (CVS), Juwan Howard's alma mater, Jones played junior varsity and ran track. But in those days, his family grew tired of raising their children in such violent surroundings. Some of his extended family explored life out in Arizona. When Tony turned 15 the summer after his freshman year of high school, the Jones family relocated to Tempe.

Jones's new Arizona high school was Marcos De Niza. His days on the highly competitive blacktop of Chicago served him well as he made De Niza's varsity as a sophomore. He also continued competing in track and field and regularly dominating the 100-meter hurdles. At six-four, and a phenomenal leaper, Jones played center but had the quickness and ball-handling ability to spend quality time on the perimeter.

Jones's senior season was the team's best ever. They reached the 1997 Arizona state finals and lost just two games all year. Jones and teammate Robert Davis, who went on to play at Loyola Marymount, led the way with one of the best one-two punches in the state.

While very few players could contain Jones, the SAT was able to shut him down just fine. Jones scored low and wound up attending Mesa Community College in Mesa. Mesa had a perennially ranked program and was seventh in the nation during Jones's freshman year as he put up a healthy 12 points a game—solid numbers considering Mesa's talent: Ernest Brown, a seven-footer who went on to play in the CBA, Thomas Watkins (headed for Iowa State), Nick Green, who played with Mike Bibby in high school, and Raheem Oliver from New York. Jones's sophomore Mesa squad was ranked fourth in the nation.

Good Division 1 schools took notice of Jones's ability to finish and strong defensive presence inside. Houston, Utah State, USC, and North Carolina–Wilmington all came calling. But Jones got injured in practice and missed half the season. He had a shot at signing with these schools, but they eventually passed on him, leaving him without many four-year options.

Fortunately, PT, Jones's dad, still had connections and arranged for Tony to attend Chicago State University for his junior and senior years. A Big Continent conference team, Chicago wasn't exactly a powerhouse but it was somewhere. But in Jones's junior year they won their most games ever in Division 1 competition, finishing 10–17 on the heels of Jones's 15 points and 10 boards a game.

Jones didn't get much attention from the NBA, but NBA players certainly knew who he was.

In 2001, the summer after his senior year, Jones had a brush with basketball greatness. A friend of Jones's knew some of the guys who run the famous Hoops Gym in Chicago. You only get in with an invite. Jones and college teammate Ernest Brown got in. It was basketball heaven. Corey Maggette, Darius Miles, Quentin Richardson, Michael Finley, Antoine Walker, and His Airness himself, Michael Jordan, were regulars at the time. Rashard Phillips (University of Detroit), Jason and Jarron Collins (Stanford, then New Jersey Nets and Utah Jazz, respectively), and Gerald Wallace (Alabama, then Sacramento Kings) were some of the top younger players.

Initially, Jones bounced around on different Hoops Gym teams, but after a few weeks, Michael Jordan took a liking to Jones and invited him to play on his team.

"That's the best run I've had in my lifetime," said Jones. "That's the best run you're going to get anywhere in America. In the world, probably. It was ridiculous. The amount of talent and

the amount of people that were there every day to play basketball was crazy. People on the sidelines, Shawn Marion, I mean everybody. If you weren't playing, there was at least 40, 50 people, and half of those people were in the NBA, just watching.

"I was playing against Jordan a lot the first couple of weeks. And I was putting it out there, I was up there killing. I was a long two-guard that could shoot, that could jump, that could handle the ball, decent enough to play the game. Jordan saw in me what he hadn't seen in a lot of guys that were in the draft. He took the opportunity to help me out, because I wasn't in any NBA predraft camps. I didn't get invited to Portsmouth, the Desert Classic, or Moody Bible, pretty much because I went to a small school that didn't go anywhere, didn't stand out. So he took it upon himself to help me out and bring me into the Wizards summer league."

Jones gained summer-league experience and also worked out with Toronto and Memphis. He expected to attend Washington's vet camp but Washington traded for forward Bobby Simmons, who Jones believes took his roster spot. From that point on, opportunities to play in the NBDL, overseas for low pay, and for the Harlem Globetrotters came and went. Jones spent the next few years working out, playing, and improving his game with good friends Ray Weathers and Jamal Livingston. Weathers, who played with NBA summer-league teams and overseas and has put up huge CBA stats, is said by Jones to be the best player in the world not in the NBA. The three friends are all shooting guards and worked together incessantly to keep improving.

Jones became "Go Get It" shortly before the summer of 2003. During an LA Fitness gym game, Jones took a lob pass and twisted, turned, and threw down a sick alley-oop. Everyone went nuts. Afterward, friends insisted that he needed a nickname. Jones actually came up with "Go Get It" himself, and the name was met with approval. From that point on, Jones kept using the nickname. Eventually, Duke Tango gave it his stamp of approval.

"To me this kid really can go get, meaning when you throw

the lob anywhere, even if it's a bad pass, he can go get it," said Tango, the nickname-meister.

With the 2003 summer AND 1 Mix Tape Tour starting, Eric "Spinmaster" Holmes, a friend of Jones's, talked to AND 1 and got them to sign Jones to a six-game minicontract. Playing against the AND 1 team, Jones's first game in Tacoma at the beginning of the tour was a success. "I was supposed to go through Phoenix and then get off the tour. That was going to be my six game contract. But basically we were opposing team players, so we had to make the game interesting, that's what we were here to do, play against them and give them some type of competition. That's basically all I was doing, was playing ball. For those first three or four games, we started a ruckus because we were killing them. We were killing the AND 1 team, plain and simple. I guess they'd never been beat like that and they saw an interest in me because I was like the main guy that was giving them problems. I was dunking, lobs, shooting, whatever, everything. I was just playing ball."

The sixth game of the tour was in Phoenix, Jones's hometown. He expected things to end there, and dropped his stuff off at home before heading to the actual event. But that day, AND 1 player relations director Maurice Elrod met with Jones and invited him to play the entire tour. Agreed. Jones played every 2003 game and solidified himself as one of the best dunkers around regardless of level. Some even call him the best dunker in the street game.

That's what they say when you can go get it.

To see more of GO GET IT, check out:

- AND 1 Mix Tape Vol. 7
- Season 2 of ESPN's *StreetBall: The AND 1 Mix Tape Tour*

Anthony Heyward
Half-Man Half-Amazing
TOUR DEBUT: 2000

Anthony Heyward, aka "Half-Man Half-Amazing," was born August 21, 1970, in Brooklyn, New York, en route to the hospital, in a taxicab, between Bedford-Stuyvesant and Crown Heights. He's lived in Brooklyn his entire life and his gritty game shows it.

Heyward got a late start, not picking up the game until he was 14. One day Heyward was walking with his cousin by 256 park in Bed-Stuy, got invited to play some ball, and was hooked on the game.

The teenage Heyward balled everywhere. Besides 256 park, he hit Kingston, Lafayette Garden, Tillary Park, Waygate Park; everywhere he could find a game he'd go.

Heyward was a five-tool player, a do-everything specialist who accepted any role anyone would offer him, just so he could be on a basketball court. He took his love for the game to Telecommunication Arts and Technology, in Bay Ridge, Brooklyn. He played only two years of high-school basketball—his freshman and junior years. "I'm not going to say I was a knucklehead, but I was kind of mischievous," he said. "So that kept me off the team every now and then. And actually, I wasn't that good. It was a learning process." An "incident" in high school that Heyward prefers not to elaborate on forced him off the team on one occasion.

Heyward graduated from high school in 1989. At the time Heyward was coming out of high school, New York City was ripe with great young basketball players, so he didn't get many college looks. He went to Farmingdale Community College in Long Island, though things didn't exactly work out. He met a guy named Les Pilgram who would eventually become a mentor and surrogate father to him. Les saw Heyward playing in Lafayette Garden, checked him out there and at other parks, and eventually asked Heyward if he was interested in going back to college. Heyward was, but didn't think colleges would take him. But with Les's help, Heyward got into Pratt Institute and began to elevate his game.

Heyward spent three years at Pratt, didn't graduate, but in 2002 returned to school, enrolling at Medgar Evers College in Crown Heights, Brooklyn, to complete his degree.

Back in the day Heyward was known as Biz. But his current famous nickname, Half-Man Half-Amazing, came from Duke Tango in 1992. Charles Jones brought Heyward to Rucker Park, to play for Mousey's Dream Team. "Nobody knew who this skinny kid from Brooklyn was," Heyward said. "But at that time, I had gotten a lot better." In his second or third game ever at Rucker,

Heyward was going a bit nuts, dunking repeatedly, including one on a 6-10 guy that prompted Duke Tango to announce to the crowd, "Oh no, he's no longer Biz, he's Half Man Half-Amazing!" Heyward loved the nickname, and kept it. Sorry, Vince. You're about six years too late.

Duke actually gave Heyward two names, Half-Man Half-Amazing and The Meteor Man, for when Heyward got upset on the court and went crazy diving for loose balls. But Meteor flamed out and Half-Man stuck.

One of the most memorable

games of Heyward's life was at Rucker Park in 1995. He was a playing for Mousey, a well-known Rucker coach, whose team battled Bad Boy's team. Mousey's Dream Team was, in Heyward's words, "a bunch of blue chips, a bunch of unknown hard workers." Along with Heyward, Dream Team featured Main Event, Wolverine, Kareem "The Best Kept Secret" Reid, and other locals.

Meanwhile Bad Boy brought recent number-one NBA draft pick Joe Smith to anchor a well-stacked squad of local legends. "But we didn't care," Heyward said. "We're on the court with them so that means we're just as good as they were. I would have to say till this day, from my experience, it was probably the greatest game that's been played in my generation." Dream Team won by two. Joe Smith had a monster game before fouling out. Nobody expected Dream Team to have a chance. "The game was just back and forth, bucket for bucket, blocked shot for blocked shot, dunk for dunk, whatever you can do, we can do, too," Heyward said. "It was a basketball player's wet dream."

"Main had like 30 points. I had like 30 and 25 rebounds. Wolverine, who was about six-eight with a 42-, 43-inch vertical, had eight blocked shots. He actually blocked one of Joe Smith's shots and threw it out the park. Threw it out the park."

Half-Man was one of the original six that played in the Linden game that got the ball rolling back in 1999. The world outside New York was first introduced to Half-Man when he infamously called out Vince Carter in a 2000 AND 1 commercial. The spot was a black-and-white Mix Tape–inspired commercial where Half-

Man sat in the back of a limo surrounded by his boys and spoke the now-famous words. "When you come in the hood, things change," Half-Man boasted. And with that the world was introduced via television commercial to the brash phenomenon that was the Mix Tape Tour.

His gravelly voice has become one of leadership for the club in the last five years. His hops may have slightly decreased but his influence on younger players hasn't.

"I try to pass on what knowledge I have to younger guys," said Heyward. "But even though I'm in the golden age of my career I'm not ready to go yet. There are still heads to crack and rebounds to grab. I'm going to leave on my own terms."

For Heyward, life after basketball will revolve around kids. He teaches fourth- and fifth-grade special education at PS 398 in Brooklyn. But until he's ready to become Mr. Heyward full-time, streetball is what matters.

"I think that thing that helped me stay at the top in terms of streetball is my relentlessness, my aggressiveness," said Heyward. "I don't care who you are. I don't care what you've done or who you've done it to, you're playing me now. Maybe something's going to change today. I play center a lot, for a lot of teams. So a lot of centers look at me and size me up and think it's going to be a cakewalk for them. So I use that to my advantage. When we start playing you'll find out I'm a little bit stronger than I look. I don't mind banging with you. I'm a durable type of guy. And at the end of the game, 9 times out of 10 I'm going to earn my respect. I don't back down from anybody."

So what's the most important lesson this teacher can impart?

"I don't prejudge anybody. The worst guy on the court could probably bust your ass on any given day. So I take no one for granted. I come out ready to bust your ass, because you must do it to me. It's streetball."

To see more of HALF-MAN HALF-AMAZING, check out:

- AND 1 Mix Tape Vol. 1
- AND 1 Mix Tape Vol. 2
- AND 1 Mix Tape Vol. 3
- AND 1 Mix Tape Vol. 4
- AND 1 Mix Tape Vol. 5
- AND 1 Mix Tape Vol. 6
- AND 1 Mix Tape Vol. 7
- AND 1 Ball Access: The Mix Tape Tour
- Season 1 of ESPN's *StreetBall: The AND 1 Mix Tape Tour*
- Season 2 of ESPN's *StreetBall: The AND 1 Mix Tape Tour*

Antoine Howard
Flash

TOUR DEBUT: 2001

On March 13, 2004, Antoine "Flash" Howard of the AND 1 Mix Tape team passed from this life. He left behind a mother, younger brother, daughter, and a world of basketball fans who will sorely miss his easy-going sense of humor and wide smile. AND 1 first happened on the six-two leaper with a magnetic personality at the courts located at 63rd and Hayes on the Southside of Chicago. Flash's energy and devotion to his friends and family have been a staple of the Mix Tape Tour for the last several years. The people who knew him best reflect on his life with fond memories.

"Flash was such a cool guy that everybody just loved to be around. I still remember the first time I met him. It was at the Chicago game during the first tour. He was on the opposing team and there was something about him. He was really good at keeping the mood light on the tour even when we'd be out on the road for weeks and everyone was dead tired. One of the things that was special about him was that every week he called everybody on the team to see how they were doing. He didn't want anything, he just wanted to know that you were all right." **—AO**

"Flash was one of those guys that I always wanted to be around. We used to laugh and talk quite a bit. Some of my best memories on the tour are of sitting in the back of the bus just joking around with Flash. He was really humble and got along with everybody. He was just a wonderful person. I've got his jersey framed on my wall." **—Duke Tango, Tour MC**

"Flash had the kind of personality where if you were in a room with about 8 to 10 people, you wouldn't know he was in the room, because he was that cool. But when he left, you would know when he was gone. That's the type of person Flash was. He was a cool, laid-back kind of guy but at the same time he still had a strong personality. And I can say this: Not one person I know had anything bad to say about Flash. There were situations where we had to help Flash where we got more upset than he did, because Flash is not that type of person. He was never looking for a conflict, but he was always there to back you up if you needed him. I love Flash like my little brother. There was nothing I wouldn't have done for him. It was unfortunate that he had to leave us. I'm going to make sure that Flash is remembered for as long as I can. Just put in a quote that Half-Man Half-Amazing loves Flash. Just put that in there for me, so I can have that immortalized." **—Half-Man Half-Amazing**

"I was very close to Flash so his passing affected me deeply. We were in this thing together and we always planned on staying together. I can remember laying back chilling on the Cayman Islands where Flash and I were talking about how big streetball was going to be, that we were gonna blow this thing up. But God took someone away from us who was a really positive person. It was his time to be called away. Even when things got the worst for him he always kept a positive frame of mind. He lived life like he knew his was going to be short. Like he knew he had to cherish every second. Flash is the kind of guy who thought about life often. Sometimes he would just leave the hotel and take long walks. He'd be gone for like two hours at a time. When we were in Paris last year we were standing out front of our hotel when we caught a glimpse of the Eiffel Tower. We just started to walk

toward it. We walked for an hour just talking about life and trying to get closer to the Eiffel Tower. Two hours later we finally got there and in that time we bonded even tighter. But we were walking forever so we decided to take a cab back. At his funeral I was honored to sing "To God Be the Glory." I hadn't planned on singing that day but his fiancée asked me if I would. She told me that she and Flash wanted me to sing at their wedding. She wanted me to sing for Flash one last time and it was a great honor for me." **—Sik Wit It**

"Flash always kept me laughing. His sense of humor always had a way of keeping everybody loose on tour. He would always give me encouragement when it came to my individual matchups. Some day I'd just be down and everyone would be coming at me. Flash would always be like, 'What you gonna do now, Sauce? It's about that time.' He just always had a way of pumping me up. That was just him. He loved to see other people doing well. I'm going to miss him forever." **—Hot Sauce**

To see more of FLASH, check out:

- AND 1 Mix Tape Vol. 5
- AND 1 Mix Tape Vol. 6
- AND 1 Mix Tape Vol. 7
- AND 1 Ball Access: The Mix Tape Tour
- Season 1 of ESPN's *StreetBall: The AND 1 Mix Tape Tour*
- Season 2 of ESPN's *StreetBall: The AND 1 Mix Tape Tour*

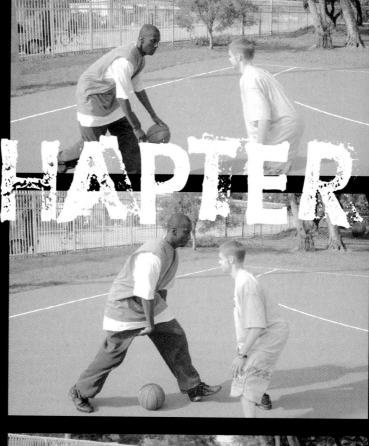

CHAPTER 5

The
Moves

egardless of where your game is or what competition level you play against, improving your skills should be the constant goal of every ballplayer. Whether you're a regular at the local gym or playground or a former intramural star looking to get back in the game, this chapter lays out step-by-step instructions, from pulling off a simple layup to the show-stopping moves the best streetballers in the world use to excite fans on the AND 1 Mix Tape Tour.

Start with the basics (even if it's just a refresher course) to get a feel for the fundamentals. Get the simple behind-the-back passes and dribbles down before you move on to really getting tricky with the ball. Mastering the basics is essential to stepping up to the kinds of tricks that you will want to have in your arsenal if you happen to find yourself at an open run.

Getting the moves in this section down will take tons of practice and game time trial and error. Chances are you'll be turning the ball over quite a bit before you master some of these moves. After you get comfortable enough with a trick, try it on one of your hoop buddies in the driveway or an empty gym. After that, only if you're ready, try it in the flow of a real pickup game. You'll find out quickly what works for you and when you can pull it off.

Mastering the moves in this chapter will make you a highly skilled streetball player. Whether you become a legend is up to you.

The Basics

You wouldn't try the Sauce 2k without mastering a simple ball fake. These are the building blocks of the game. Study. Perfect. School. If you're an advanced baller, brush up anyway.

The Perfect J

Square your feet shoulder-width apart. Jump straight up and land in the same spot.

1.

Raise the ball just above your head. This will be your release point, so be careful not to bring the ball too far back.

2.

It's a basketball, not a shotput, so flick your wrist to release the ball. Follow through every time.

3.

Close Up

This is what you look like to a defender. Your fingertips are the only part of your shooting hand to touch the ball. When you begin your release, your guide hand should automatically fall away.

Again. Follow through. Your arm should look like you're trying to make a goose shadow puppet. Repeat 1,000 times. Or until dinner.

Left Fade Away

No player's repertoire should be without this move. Don't show up on any court without it.

Catch the ball in the post. **1.**

2. Hold your pivot (right) foot and turn hard toward the left baseline.

Square your feet and rise up for the jumpshot.

Fading away slightly will make it almost impossible for even a taller defender to block your shot.

3. 4.

177

Up and Under

This move will expand your rep in the post. Think Kevin McHale.

Catch the ball in the post and shoulder fake left. **1.**

2. Turn the opposite way on your right (pivot) foot.

3.

Pump fake quickly as if you you're going to shoot a fadeaway.

4. With your defender in the air, explode by him.

5. If you can get to the rim without dribbling, that's a bonus.

6. Finish strong.

179

Spin Move

A staple. A must-learn move.

Start off in the triple threat.

1.

Rock a low right-to-left crossover.

2.

With the ball safely in your left hand you can begin your spin.

3.

Now your right foot is your pivot. Spin hard. Stay on the balls of your feet to maintain balance.

4.

Drop the ball out in front of you as you complete your spin. There will be a moment you won't have contact with the ball, so make sure you keep it low and close to your body so you don't get swiped.

5.

Pick the ball back up with your right hand. As always, keep your head up.

6.

Finger Roll

George Gervin could finger roll. So can Sauce. You better learn too.

1.

As you enter the lane, keep the ball high above your head for takeoff.

2.

As you glide toward the rim, rotate the ball so the back of your hand is facing the rim.

3.

To release the ball, let it roll off your fingertips while flipping it up and over the rim.

Floater

This is a nice tool if you're not great at finishing at the rim

By the time you've reached the foul line you've already picked up your dribble.

1.

Although you're taking off of one foot, bring the ball up as if you were shooting a jumpshot.

2.

Note that with this closeup you can't tell whether Professor is about to shoot a jump-shot or a floater.

3.

Keep your body relatively balanced; release the ball like you would a jumper. As always, follow through.

4.

Stiff Leg

This is a crossover you can use when the defender is crowding you. Unlike a regular crossover, this is one the defender won't see coming.

Start with a right-hand dribble as if you were going to drive hard to your right.

1.

Stop short with your left leg. Keep the ball low.

2.

When you stop short, the defender will fall back, giving you space to get your shot off.

3.

With the ball in your left hand, the defender will be frozen in his tracks if he isn't already on his butt.

4.

You're off to the races.

5.

183

One Hand Behind the Back

The object here is to go around your body using just one hand. You'll thank us the next time you're in a tight spot.

Start with a left-hand (or right-hand) dribble, bring the ball across your body, and dribble it behind your right leg.

1.

Quickly reach back around with your left hand to continue the dribble.

2.

With a fluid motion, bring the ball back to your start position.

3.

Repeat steps 1 and 2.

4.

Note: This is a nice move to use as you bring the ball up the floor to set up a variety of moves.

Off Da Foot

Here's a quick move to throw in between tricks to keep your rhythm. Think of it as a ball fake with your foot.

Start off with a low dribble in front of the body.

1.

Bring the dribble to a stop on your foot. As you lift your foot, keep your hand on top of the ball.

2.

On your down-stroke, pull your foot away to keep your dribble alive.

3.

Off Da Head

If your man is sleeping, wake him up.

1.

Start with a low dribble similar to Off Da Foot.

2.

Raise up with a high dribble and tap the ball quickly off your defender's face. Make sure you get his forehead (around the hairline), so the ball will bounce back cleanly.

Pick-N-Roll

Not all streetball is isolation. This is essential to any two-man game. Use it well.

Run your man into a solid pick. (If you're setting the pick, cross your arms in front of you below your waist, hold your ground, and be tough.)

1.

Your man is stuck. Push hard with the dribble.

2.

As the pick setter begins to turn, make sure your defender hasn't fought his way through the pick.

3.

As you begin to drive the lane, your teammate is beginning to cut toward the hoop.

4.

Chances are you'll get picked up by another defender. If you don't, pop the J. If someone steps out, simply drop a pass off to the cutter.

5.

6.

Two steps later...

7.

...someone gets flushed on.

187

Behind-the-Back Low Dribble

Purely show, this is something you can put your man to sleep with.

 **1.**

 **2.**

 **3.**

Spread your feet as wide as you can without doing the splits.

Rock the dribble back and forth behind your back with your hands no more than shoulder-width apart.

Get the ball up to speed back and forth. Use your fingertips only. Keep it low.

Note: This is a position you might not be able to get out of quickly.

Ball Trick

You won't be able to pull this in a game, but it should impress your friends.

Make sure the ball rises a few feet above your head.

2.

Stand as if you are about to shoot a free throw. Bounce the ball.

1.

As the ball drops, crouch forward to catch the ball on your back. Time your crouch as the ball hits to prevent it from bouncing.

 **3.**

Intermediate
Skills

Fake Behind-the-Back Dribble

Here's a nice little move you can use to connect tricks.

Go through your legs from left to right.

1.

With the ball in your right hand, begin the wrap-around as if you were throwing a behind-the-back pass.

2.

Instead of throwing a pass, wrap the ball around your right leg.

3.

Balance the ball.

4.

Regain the dribble with your right hand.

4.

189

Boomerang

Purely for crowd reaction. Pull it off and your friends will worship you.

Load up with the ball in your right hand.

1.

Note: Here's where you need to pay attention.

2. Whip off a quick in-and-out dribble.

3. Bring the ball forward as if you were going to wing a shovel pass.

4. This is what it looks like when you bring the ball forward. The key is to cuff your hand behind the ball.

5. Just before you release the ball, turn your wrist inward and snap the ball straight up in the air.

Note 2: This is almost impossible. If you fail to master this move, don't be surprised.

6. This is what your follow-through will look like. Note that Hot Sauce keeps an eye on the ball as it flies up.

7. When the ball comes back down, continue your dribble.

Double Trouble

This is just a little something to get the place jumpin' before you get into your moves.

1. Rock a few back-and-forth low crossovers to set this one up.

2. Bring the ball slowly from left to right.

3. Tap the ball with the bottom of your foot to keep the dribble alive. Don't stomp on the ball, just tap it.

4. Alternate with your opposite foot. Repeat.

5. Reset your dribble.

Around-the-World Dribble K ids, be like Alimoe!

Keep your dribble low as you approach your defender.

1.

Go between the legs from right to left.

2.

When your dribble is in your left hand, cuff it and swing it over his head.

3.

4.

Now the ball is all the way across your body.

5.

Drop the ball directly behind your back with a behind-the-back dribble.

6.

Now the ball is back in your left hand, setting up your next move.

Step-Back Baseline J

Don't show up without this, or you'll be sent home early.

Catch the ball in the post. **1.**

Keeping your left foot as your pivot, turn toward the right baseline and pump fake the shot. You should be square with the side of the rim. **2.**

Go directly from the pump fake to a behind-the-back dribble. **3.**

With the ball in your left hand you can penetrate left, but hold it... **4.**

...simply pull up for the jump shot. **5.**

Breathe and Stop

This is one of Hot Sauce's favorite moves. Use it against him, because even he can't stop it.

Set up your man with a few back-and-forth dribbles.

1.

As you go back and forth you don't want to fall asleep yourself, so be alert.

2.

With the ball in your right hand, bang a quick cross to the left, as if you were about to penetrate hard.

3.

With the ball high in your left hand...

4.

...simply drop it off and reach over with your right hand to catch it.

5.

After you catch the ball, lunge forward as if you're headed left, then stop hard with your right foot.

6.

Bring the ball back to your start position.

7.

Since this is streetball, you've still got your dribble. But don't let your high-school coach catch you doing this one.

8.

Kick Through the Legs

This is a little variation on throwing the ball through your man's legs.

Crouch down and rock a low back-and-forth dribble. The closer you are to your man the better.

Set the ball down in front of you. Keep your hand on top of it initially, so the ball won't bounce back up.

Lightly kick the ball forward through your defender's legs. (Just a tap will do. You'll want to keep it on the ground.)

1.

2.

3.

Run around your defender to retrieve the ball. It helps to first jab in one direction, then cut the opposite way. If the defender turns in the same direction as you run by, it will be harder to get back to the ball.

4.

5.

Pick up the ball and regain your dribble.

Advanced
Moves

Elbow Pass

Just another way to get the ball from point A to point B.

Bring the ball around your back, as if you were making a behind-the-back pass.

1.

Instead of tossing a pass, place the ball just below your shoulder blades.

2.

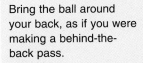

Knock the ball to an open teammate with your elbow. Look away to add flair.

3.

Professor Midterm Fail this and there's no shame. Master it and move to the head of the class.

Casually cross over from right to left.

1.

Keep the ball low and your feet set so you don't tip off the defender.

2.

Raise slightly and pause. The defender will have no idea where you're going.

3.

Pull off hard with your right foot.

4.

Slam on the brakes hard by planting your right foot.

5.

Quickly dribble a low left-to-right dribble between the legs.

6.

Cross your body with the ball from left to right by cuffing it.

7.

Make sure your hand is on top of the ball.

8.

Drop the ball back through your legs with enough zip that you won't get plucked.

9.

Now the ball is back in your left hand and your options are unlimited.

10.

Sauce Zit

Here's one of Hot Sauce's signature moves. Get the rhythm down and try to pull this one off as fast as you can. Watch the Mix Tapes and you'll know why.

Dribble from left to right with a between-the-legs dribble from back to front.

1.

With the ball in your right hand, cuff it and bring it forward as if you're going to toss an underhand pass.

2.

Pull the ball back, still cuffed, as if you're going to regain your dribble.

3.

Quickly, bring the ball again across your body. With your left leg forward, dribble the ball through your legs from left to right.

4.

Reach back with your right hand (the same

5.

6.

You've got your dribble back. What you do

Now You See It

They've been doing this since the Linden game. See Mix Tape Vol. 2.

Start in the triple-threat position.

1.

Push off your left foot as if you're going to drive right.

2.

Toss the ball out a few feet to your right side like you would fake a pass. The trick is to put enough backspin on the ball so that it comes back to you.

3.

With the back-spin you've put on the ball, let it bounce behind your body.

4.

5.

Simply pick the ball up with your left hand.

Go into your next move.

6.

Off-the-Knee Alley-Oop

If you can pull this one off, call AND 1 immediately.

Pick up your dribble near the foul line. (You'll want to practice this one closer to the hoop.) Set up the ball with both hands as if you are a punter.

1.

2.

Drop the ball on your knee and knee it to where you would normally throw an alley-oop. It will take a ton of practice to get the ball to go straight.

Remember to slow down enough to maintain your balance. Since this pass originates low, make sure there is enough space between you and your defender.

3.

4.

Your job is done. Add a look away for extra flair.

Now it's up to your man...

5. **6.**

...to finish strong.

emember, fundamentals are the foundation of any form of basketball, from streetball to the NBA. They are the building blocks of any move, be it textbook or street style. Without them you might as well close this book. Before and after you practice your street moves, work on some fundamental drills like dribbling through cones (or whatever you can find) with your head up, dribbling two balls at the same time, and doubling your efforts with your weak hand.

The more time you spend in the gym or on the blacktop honing your ability, the more comfortable you will become with the ball in your hands. Improved dribbling, passing, and penetration will be an offshoot of your confidence with the basketball. The stronger your fundamentals are, the stronger your game will be. Go practice.

Epilogue:

Catching Up with
Rafer Alston

Geraldine Alston sat in her apartment in New York City with tears streaming down her face. Her son Rafer had caused tears in the past, but this was different. These were the joyous kind. All her attention was focused on her 27-inch television and the madness of a postgame celebration that played out before her. With 0.5 seconds remaining on the clock her son had just drilled the game-winning shot to lift the Miami Heat over the Dallas Mavericks 119–118. Geraldine, her husband, Steve Elerby, and her eldest son, Ramar, jumped about and screamed at the top of their lungs when Rafer dropped in an off-balance leaner from the left baseline.

"We were making so much noise I thought the landlord was going to tell us to get out," said Geraldine. "But I didn't care because I was just so happy."

Happy her son had made it after so many years of having to scratch and claw his way through. After jail, bad press, and the street rep that made him famous. After PS 108. After Cardozo. After Ventura. After Fresno City. After Fresno State. And especially after George Karl and the Milwaukee Bucks.

"I've had some tough times trying to get where I am," said Skip. "Anybody that knows me knows that all I ever wanted was a chance. An opportunity. Now that I finally got it, I'm making it work."

Before the 2003–04 NBA season Pat Riley offered Rafer a one-year contract with the Miami Heat. Play well and we'll see what happens. But Riley had no idea the kid from Queens would be one of the driving forces that steered the Heat back toward the playoffs for the first time in four years.

The fifth-year point guard ran his team's offense as smoothly as any guard in the league, carefully protecting the basketball while doling out pinpoint assists. His 3:1 assist-to-turnover ratio was a team best. The Heat were 26–17 when Skip scored in double figures. Playing 32 minutes a night, Rafer was the only guard in the league to lead his team in assists (4.6) and steals (1.4) coming off the bench.

"When he's in there we go," said fellow Queens native Lamar Odom. "He doesn't think about who or where to get the ball, he just finds people."

In finally proving himself to front offices leaguewide, it seems Alston has done the near impossible: He has shed his street rep. Any streetballer with designs on the league will tell you the number-one reason they've been kept at bay is the undeserved rep that streetballers are undisciplined ballplayers.

"I don't know why streetball has been given such a bad rap by some people," said Skip. "There are so many guys with real skills who never come close to getting a chance. I think streetball should be embraced as a positive thing.

"On the other hand, to a certain extent my Skip to My Lou persona held me back. People classified me as strictly a trickball player, which wasn't the case. You have to understand that I earned my rep playing organized ball. I showed I could run a team at Fresno State. I've worked on my shooting and fundamentals every summer like crazy. This is what I've been about for the last 12 years. Nobody ever gave me a job because I was a good streetballer."

"It says a lot about him as a basketball player that he could leave the streetball stuff behind and play the NBA game," said Heat teammate Bimbo Coles.

Rafer can look back at his struggles and laugh. But there was a time when being tied to the end of a bench was no laughing matter. After he was drafted by Milwaukee in 1998, Rafer spent the better part of the next three seasons schooling the first team in practice and wasting away on George Karl's bench. The first time Geraldine and Steve went to see him play, Rafer didn't get off the bench. By the second half, Geraldine, who was sitting opposite the Bucks bench, left her seat, walked around the court, and stood right behind the Bucks bench where Karl was standing.

She motioned for Karl to lean over and she politely told him that they didn't come all this way to see Rafer glued to the bench. Karl was taken aback but it didn't seem to help Rafer's cause. The coach continued to ignore Skip for the rest of the year.

"We just didn't see eye to eye for some reason," said Skip.

Actually, Karl rarely saw any reason to put Skip in the game in favor of Sam Cassell. Rafer would call home after Bucks game and sadly tell his mother and his now stepfather, Steve Elerby, that he no longer wanted to be there.

"He was hurting but we kept telling him that he had to stay and fight through it," said Elerby.

After three consecutive one-year deals, Milwaukee let him go when the Bucks blew up the team in 2002. He got no offers to play but was invited to the Golden State Warriors preseason training camp. "I feel I played pretty well, but for some reason they decided not to keep me," Skip recalled. Instead they went with A.J. Guyton, who is no longer in the league.

Since he rarely got the chance to shine, no other teams inquired about his services. From there he went into a funk and was fast running out of options. He was 26 and not getting any younger. Skip felt that he shouldn't have to go down south to the NBDL, because he had already paid his dues. After Elerby convinced him that it was for the best, that nobody would pick him up if he was out of sight pouting at home, Skip made for Mobile, Alabama, and signed with the Mobile Revelers.

After just six games, in which he averaged 15.8 points, 9.7 assists, and 3.8 rebounds in 36.1 minutes, he was offered a 10-day contract by the Toronto Raptors. Now was his time. He was out from under George Karl. If he wasn't going to show his stuff now, he never was. In his first start with Toronto, he scored a career-high 20 points to go along with 8 assists, 4 rebounds, and 2 steals in 25 minutes. The fact that it came against the Bucks and Karl made it that much sweeter. Two days later he jacked his career best to 23 against the Cavaliers. He finished the season with averages of 7.8 points, 4.1 assists, and 2.3 rebounds.

When the season ended, he was once again without a team. That is, until Pat Riley came calling. "I've been saying it all along," Skip said. "All I wanted was the opportunity to be on the court and prove myself. No matter what happens from here on out, I've done that."

After an 0–7 start, Rafer found his groove and turned the Heat into one of the most exciting teams in the league while averaging career highs in every statistical category. The story of Skip to My Lou, playground legend, may live on for eternity, but the reality of Rafer Alston, NBA guard, is what he was after all along.

The Top
Streetball Courts
in the Nation

- **HOLCOMBE RUCKER PARK** (New York, N.Y.): Where it all began. From The Hawk to The Goat to The Doctor to Skip. Everybody who's anybody has played here.

- **WEST 4TH** (New York, N.Y.): Located in hipster Greenwich Village, The Cage may be the best regular run in the country and has hosted giants like Kareem Abdul-Jabbar and Tiny Archibald.

- **VENICE BEACH COURTS** (Venice, Calif.): About a hundred yards from the Pacific Ocean, the scenery is hard to beat. So is the comp.

- **ST. CECILIA** (Detroit, Mich.): Run at St. Cecilia's Catholic Church in Detroit. The finest ballplayers Michigan has ever produced (Chris Webber, Magic Johnson, Derrick Coleman) have all honed their games here.

- **RUN-N-SHOOT** (Atlanta, Ga.) (Hot Sauce's home court): It's tough to get in a game at the original run and shoot, even at two in the morning.

- **RUN-N-SHOOT** (Washington, D.C.): High socks and the DC crossover are two things that every young'un at this hoop haven is not without. Some of the best run on the East Coast.

- **THE GARDEN** (Coney Island, Brooklyn, N.Y.) (Stephon Marbury's home court): The court is in the shadow of the building that Steph and his cousin, Sebastian Telfair, grew up in. "It's the first place I made somebody fall," said Sebastian.

- **PS 44 PLAYGROUND** (Brooklyn, N.Y.): Immortalized in the hoop documentary *Soul in the Hole*. If you're lucky you just might catch seldom-seen legend Booger Smith doing his thing.

- **DREW LEAGUE** (Los Angeles, Calif.): According to Sik Wit It, it's the best run in the country. But don't show up to South Central without proper game or connections.

- **FONDÉ RECREATION CENTER** (Houston, Tex.): You're likely not ready to bang with the pros who regularly run here, but game is game, so prove yourself and you'll earn respect. Go across town to the Westside Tennis Club for the best run in the city. Oops. Sorry, if you aren't already in the league, they won't let you in the front door.

- **VICTORY PARK** (Pasadena, Calif.) (Sik's home court): when Sik wasn't killing foe at the Drew, he was practicing his handle here.

- **CONNIE MACK COURT AT 22ND AND LEHIGH** (Philly) (AO's home court): A rusted chain-link fence surrounds this slab of fabled North Philly asphalt to give you that old school playground feel. Every other kid mimicking AO's moves brings it up to date.

- **TREMIL PARK AND MERRILL PARK** (Chicago) (Flash's home court): Located on Chicago's Southside, in between fast-paced games locals dole out endless stories about Flash, who put their court on the map.

- **LAKEFRONT COURTS** (Chicago) (Go Get It's home court): On the horizon is the beautiful Chicago skyline. Behind you Lake Michigan provides ballers with enough breeze to persuade them to take it to the hole. Now you know why Chi-Town can penetrate so well.

- **4TH WARD PARK** (Linden, N.J.) (Main Event's home court): Most of the Mix Tape Vol. 2 footage came from this park. Fourth Ward Park is Linden's version of Rucker Park. If you've got game, you've played there. If you don't, you haven't.

Required Reading/ Bibliography

Hoops Nation by Chris Ballard; Owl Books, 1998

Pickup Artists by Lars Anderson and Chad Millman; Verso, 1998

Where'd You Get Those Shoes? New York City's Sneaker Culture: 1960–1987 by Bobbito Garcia; Testify, 2003

The Basketball Diaries by Jim Carroll; Penguin, 1987

The Last Shot by Darcy Frey; Mariner Books, 1992

Asphalt Gods: An Oral History of the Rucker Tournament by Vincent M. Mallozzi; Doubleday, 2003

The City Game by Pete Axthelm; University of Nebraska Press, 1999

Swee'Pea and Other Playground Legends by John Valenti and Ron Naclerio; Michael Kesend Publishing, 1990

Heaven Is a Playground by Rick Telander; University of Nebraska Press, 2002

Elevating the Game: Black Men and Basketball by Nelson George; HarperCollins, 1992

Acknowledgments

Basketball is the birthplace of all of my dreams. It's everything I am, want to be, or will become. Or something like that. That's a line from Walter McCarty's character in *He Got Game*. It sums up how thousands of kids across the country, decade after decade, feel about basketball. Myself included. But despite a 40-inch vertical and a fairly reliable J, I never made the NBA. Something tells me you can relate. But basketball in one way or another is still all of those things to me. And this book is for people who can relate.

This book is for the real ballers. The ones always trying to get next. Dudes you know. Your boy down the block. Your cousin with that wicked cross. You, with your weak left hand. For the ones who can play, and the ones who can't. Because they are out there at the parks, the gyms, and countless open runs across the country keeping the real game alive. From Rucker Park to a backboard nailed to a barn in Indiana to the courts at Magnolia Elementary in Lanham, Maryland, where I first dunked. This book is for the real ballers.

Right off I have to the thank the entire book team that struggled right along with me to make this book a reality and put it together: super agent Marc Gerald (without whom this wouldn't have been possible), Matthew Benjamin at HarperCollins, Big Mike Ellis, Mandy Murphy, Mark Edwards, Ryan Rimsnider, and the rest of the AND 1 crew. Special thanks to Geraldine Alston, Steve Elerby, and all the parents and grandparents of the AND 1 Mix Tape ballers. A huge shout-out to the photographers—Michael Schreiber, Oluwaseye Olusa, Daven Baptiste, and Pete Kuhns—for helping to take this book to the next level.

I hope you get as much out of this book as I got putting into it.

And here are the people and places I really can't forget because they show me love 24-sev (or at least most of the time) or have affected me in some way or another on my basketball journey over the years. Randolph "Butch" Childress, Jerod Mustaf and his pop Shaar, Lawrence Moten, Keith Gatlin, Len Bias, Keith Veney, Cole Field House, Central High Falcons, Owen Smith, Cree, Knot, Chewy, Terrell, Boo, and God. All my AAU and summer league coaches. All the college coaches who recruited me but never signed me.

Coach Louis Wilson, Hank Lloyd Jr. (r.i.p.), the Jordan Brand crew, Good Luck Rec Center, the Kenner League, Urban Coalition, Prince Georges County, Glen Arden Midnight League (the original), Doc's Gym, the Madness Shop, We R One, Melvin's Crab House, P.A. Palace, Foot Locker at Landover Mall, Clemont's Barbershop, Georgia Avenue, Hobart Street, all of D.C. and Shoppers Food Warehouse in Largo where I worked for eight years.

And now's as good a time as any to shout out my boys in the league who I've gotten to know over the years and who have made my experience around the game today as enjoyable as when I first started playing 33. Elton Brand, Corey Maggette, Q-Rich, D Miles, Kobe Bryant, Tracy McGrady, Andre Miller, Jamal Crawford (and cousin Gabe), Lamar Odom, Rafer Alston (and brother Ramar), Michael Redd, Jay Williams, Carmelo Anthony, Marcus Camby, DerMarr Johnson, Moochie Norris, Sebastian Telfair (and family), Dwight Howard, and Chris Paul.

Here are some more people who deserve love too: Scoop Jackson, Jeff Lenchiner at insidehoops.com, Sonny Vaccaro, Wayne Hall, Dartagnian Stamps, Kevin Samples, James White and his pops, Brian Dyke, Curtis Malone, Kevin Bradbury, Lonnie White, *ESPN* The Magazine, and everybody in the NBDL.

Can't forget all my hard working PR people, sneaker pimps, runners, AAU coaches, camp organizers, hustlers, jewelry makers, street historians, trainers, chefs, bodyguards, personal security, barbers, and orange juice guys who keep me so plugged in to the scene.

Also, I can't forget my boys at *Slam* magazine who I've been runnin' with since the tip. Much love and props to Ryan, Russ, Ben, Lang, and the rest of the *Slam* fam. Seriously, there are at least two hundred more people I can't squeeze in here. Just hit me on my cell.

But most important, I've got to thank my family for enthusiastically supporting everything I do. They are my inspiration for everything. My mother Sally (who gave me the writing gene), father Ransford, brother Geoff, sister Laura, and nephew Andrew Tyler. You guys are awesome. Finally, I'll close with the last line from season one of the *Streetball* series on ESPN. Rafer Alston was asked what became of the countless streetballers with game and little else who couldn't quite get to the "next level" and faded away. "None of them made it," he said, shaking his head and staring off into the distance. "None of them made it." He wasn't talking about me.

One,
Chris

Index

UPRISE MID

AND1

AVAILABLE AT
Foot Locker